PRAISE FOR
FOUNDATION REPAIR SECRETS

As a homeowner considers having to make a significant investment in their home, this book will be a great resource to navigate foundation assessments and repair options. Well-informed homeowners are better equipped to ask questions of the repair contractor in order to make better decisions and avoid unrealistic expectations. The more you know, the better the outcome.

Gregg A. Creaser, P.E.
President/Geotechnical Team Principal at SPEEDIE & ASSO-CIATES, Inc.

R.K. Bob Brown's book is a great resource for homeowners who want to learn how their house foundations work and make informed decisions regarding foundation repairs.

Randolph Marwig, P.E.
President Western Technologies Inc.

R. K. Bob Brown used a personal approach to explain a topic that might seem foreign to most. Using anecdotes and real life experiences, Bob shared ideas and a vision in his book, *Foundation Repair Secrets,* that will likely save a lot of people time and money on their foundation repairs.

Clint L. Mueller, P.E.

R.K. Bob Brown has created a step-by-step guide for home-owners to understand potential causes and remediation techniques for foundation and slab movement issues. *Foundation Repair Secrets* takes Bob's years of expertise in the foundation repair industry and presents them in a simplified manner for everyone to understand. It also shares what to anticipate when it comes to dealing with home foundation and slab repairs. This book makes clear not only Bob's knowledge and passion for the foundation repair industry; but also his devotion to ensuring homeowners are provided the correct repair for their individual needs.

Greg Bakkum, SE, PE

I want to express my appreciation to Arizona Foundation Solutions on how it conducts its investigations using sound engineering principals supervised by a registered professional engineer to diagnose foundation distress in lieu of a sales person performing the investigation which is commonly used around Arizona. This engineering team takes elevation and dimensional measurements, observations of distress, and they follow the procedures of a Level B Investigation as outlined in the Texas ASCE. They then take this data and compile it, analyze it before they carefully make recommendations endorsed by a professional engineer. The report provided is easy to understand, user friendly, and most importantly technically sound in judgment. As a professional licensed engineer who gets phone calls regarding foundation settlement (or heave), I endorse and recommend a method of investigation as performed by Arizona Foundation Solutions.

Anthony J. Polusny, P.E.

This book is a great, easy-to-read guide for homeowners with distressed houses in need of repair. Although distress assessments can be costly, you will likely have a better chance of a successful repair with geotechnical and structural engineers involved. Most distress results from various contributing factors that take knowledge and experience to fully understand. It is cheaper to fix the actual problem the first time, rather than hope a repair works. *Foundation Repair Secrets* provides some basic knowledge for the homeowner to make informed decisions on one of their biggest investments.

Chet L. Pearson, P.E.
Arizona

FOUNDATION
REPAIR SECRETS

R.K. BOB BROWN

FOUNDATION REPAIR SECRETS

LEARN HOW TO PROTECT YOURSELF AND SAVE THOUSANDS

Advantage | Books

Published by Advantage, Charleston, South Carolina.
Member of Advantage Media.

ADVANTAGE is a registered trademark, and the Advantage colophon is a trademark of Advantage Media Group, Inc.

Printed in the United States of America.

10 9 8 7 6 5 4 3 2 1

ISBN: 978-1-64225-638-3 (Hardcover)
ISBN: 978-1-64225-637-6 (eBook)

LCCN: 2022921184

Cover design by Matthew Morse.
Layout design by Megan Elger.

This publication is designed to provide accurate and authoritative information in regard to the subject matter covered. It is sold with the understanding that the publisher is not engaged in rendering legal, accounting, or other professional services. If legal advice or other expert assistance is required, the services of a competent professional person should be sought.

Advantage Media helps busy entrepreneurs, CEOs, and leaders write and publish a book to grow their business and become the authority in their field. Advantage authors comprise an exclusive community of industry professionals, idea-makers, and thought leaders. Do you have a book idea or manuscript for consideration? We would love to hear from you at **AdvantageMedia.com**.

*For Cindy, whose support has enabled me to
focus my energies for so many years.*

CONTENTS

ABOUT THE AUTHOR

R. K. Bob Brown graduated in 1984 from Arizona State University with a bachelor of design science from the school of architecture and a bachelor of science from the school of business in finance. In 1988, Bob founded Arizona Repair Masons Inc., and Arizona Foundation Solutions in 2001 and has been operating them since. Bob brings more than thirty years of construction experience and is LEED accredited. He is International Concrete Repair Institute moisture-measurement certified and is one of two Certified Foundation Repair Specialists (CFRSs) in the state of Arizona. CFRS is a designation of the Foundation Repair Association. Bob completed the grouting fundamentals course from the Colorado School of Mines in 2009. He has served as an expert witness in court cases on several occasions and is the holder of four patents. He is Level 1 certified by the Post-Tensioning Institute, is an EPA-certified radon measurement and mitigation specialist, and provides continuing education as an Arizona Department of Real Estate–approved CEU provider.

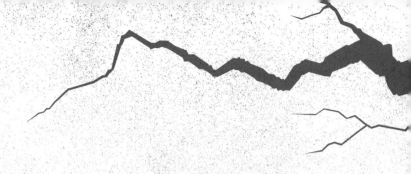

GLOSSARY OF TERMS USED IN THIS BOOK

ABC: Aggregate base course. A sand-and-gravel layer placed below concrete.

BACKFILL: Soil placed back after being excavated. It will usually compress or consolidate over time.

CEMENT: A component of concrete made from calcium, a plentiful element thanks to all of the lobsters and other crustaceans whose remains are calcified by the oceans. It is transformed by extreme heat and ground to a fine powder. The ancient Romans first used natural pozzolana cooked from the volcano of Mount Vesuvius.

CLAY SOIL: Distinguished by its tiny and varied mineral particles, clay has a negative charge and is attracted to water that has a positive charge. There are several mineral compositions of clay (kaolinite, illite, montmorillonite, etc.). The result, known as clay suction, causes many types of clay to swell when exposed to water. Montmorillonite can expand as much as 10 percent when exposed to water (a little more than eight feet of this material in the soil could heave ten inches!).

CENTER HEAVE: Heaving in the center of a foundation. Sometimes called dome heave.

COLD JOINT: An area between two portions of concrete that were placed at different times. It has no continuous integrity (can easily move separately).

COLLAPSIBLE SOIL: Usually sands and silt (larger than clay soil particles) that can consolidate when exposed to water or sometimes just the overburden of weight of something on top of it.

COMPACTION GROUTING: A technique that can fill sinkholes or level sinking foundations by injecting a cementlike substance deep into the ground to fill voids and compact the soil at those deeper levels.

COMPRESSION: In the context of this book, strengthening concrete so it can bear more weight. A concrete foundation with steel cables that are tensioned (pulled tight) after the concrete is placed will gain compressive strength to bear the load and tensile strength to hold together.

CONCRETE: Invented by the ancient Romans, a common form of pavement made up of sand, rocks, cement, and water. When combined, a chemical reaction occurs and transforms those ingredients into a solid material.

CUT: In soil nomenclature, the act of excavating soil to create a level surface for construction.

DEFLECTION: Deviation from a straight line. Usually meant to show evidence of problems from differential movement.

EDGE HEAVE: Heaving on the edge of a foundation as opposed to center heave or dome heave.

EVAPOTRANSPIRATION: The cycle of water vapor returning to the atmosphere from soil and bodies of water.

FILL: In soil nomenclature, the act of adding soil to level out a site for construction.

FLOOR-LEVEL SURVEY: Also known as a manometer survey, the measurement and recording for analysis of floor elevations or heights to help determine settlement or heave.

FLOOR SLAB: The concrete placed in the floor of a house. In conventional foundations, it is not a part of the foundation system other than holding up non-roof-bearing interior walls.

FOOTING: The part of a foundation that lies on top of the soil to provide support for loads above it.

GEOTECHNICAL: As a branch of civil engineering, it involves the science of soil mechanics and can overlap with structural engineering, which usually deals with things above the ground.

HEAVE: In the context of this book, expansive soil swelling—usually upward—that occurs when certain types of clay soil are wetted. Often this can be cyclical with wet and dry seasons or, conversely, accumulative in the case of long-term moisture under foundations.

HELICAL PILE: A steel pile that is advanced into the soil by screwing into the ground to provide foundational support.

MUD JACKING: The process of raising slabs by injecting pressurized grout or polyurethane foam (see *polyurethane* below) under them.

NOMENCLATURE: The terms commonly used by an industry or field, such as some of the words in this glossary.

POLYURETHANE: A type of chemical that can be catalyzed by water or by other chemicals. It has many forms and uses. Some love water (hydrophilic), and some eschew it (hydrophobic). Some swell when reacting; others simply gel and harden. They usually react faster than epoxy chemical reactions.

POST-TENSIONED SLAB: Concrete foundation with steel cables that are tensioned (pulled tight) after the concrete is placed to increase the stiffness of the concrete.

PUSH PILE: A steel pile that is advanced into the soil using hydraulic cylinders using the house or structure as a reactive force.

REFUSAL: In pile installation, this is the point at which the pile encounters hard-enough soil to refuse advancing, given a precalculated driving force.

SETTLEMENT: In the context of this book, when a structure sinks into the ground.

SERVICEABILITY: A description of damage on a structure (cosmetic or structural), such as reoccurring cracks, doors, and windows that don't open properly and other dysfunctions.

SPREAD FOOTINGS: A building foundation base made of concrete. These surround a typical conventional foundation, supporting the roof bearing walls by spreading out the load, but typically don't hold the slab down.

STEM WALL: A small wall that sits on top of the footing to support the frame or masonry wall above it.

STRATUM OR STRATA: A distinct layer of soil, usually one of many. Each layer can consist of different mineral content, density, and water content.

TOPOGRAPHY: The mapping of a surface, usually with lines to show elevation differences.

UNDERPINNING: Driving or screwing piles down through the soil layers until they meet strong resistance. It's like putting the house on stilts so it can be releveled.

FOREWORD

Foundation distress in a home can be extremely traumatic to homeowners. In some cases, mitigation costs to a homeowner can exceed the original cost of a home. Foundation repair costs each year across the United States are more than the combined damage from tornadoes, hurricanes, earthquakes, and floods. Insurance companies know this and typically exclude coverage for foundation distress resulting from moisture-sensitive soil movements. Homeowners with foundation problems are keen to get expensive mitigation performed as economically and correctly as possible without sacrificing quality.

I am a senior civil engineer with forty years of forensic geotechnical experience on thousands of projects in Arizona. Much of my work involves the review of excessive soil movements and foundation failures. Many of these cases include failures of previous repair attempts. I have worked with this book's author, R.K. Bob Brown, and his company Arizona Foundation Solutions (AFS) on dozens of soil movement mitigation projects over the last fifteen years. I also helped review aspects of AFS's patented MoistureLevel System®.

Typical problem soils in Arizona include expansive clays, compressible and collapsible soils, and inadequately compacted fill.

Moisture changes in these soils can cause heave, settlement, and shrinkage. Dry climate conditions in the desert portions of Arizona aggravate soil moisture extremes, which can result in damaging soil movements. Wet soil moisture conditions followed by droughts in higher elevations in Arizona contribute to cyclic soil movements and resultant distress in homes.

Foundation repair companies and specialized structural and geo-technical engineers work to identify the cause of soil movements and to prescribe mitigation. The goal is to stabilize current soil movements and reduce future distress under the home. Unfortunately, there can be a misdiagnosis of the soil problem, leading to inappropriate, excessive, or unneeded mitigation. It is quite common for repair con-tractors to treat a home diagnosed as having settling soil with piers and grouting. When it turns out that the problem was the drying shrinkage of expansive clay soils or the swelling of expansive clays, the piers and grout can make distress conditions worse if the expansive clay soils become additionally wetted.

Structural and geotechnical engineers go through classic soil mechanics classes in college that help to identify types of problem soils, but there is little formal education on what to do to reduce the impact of damaging moisture-sensitive soil movements under a home after the original construction. In many cases the only precaution that geotechnical engineers offer in the original geotechnical recom-mendations is to "control moisture changes in foundation soils." This is easy to say but hard to do in actual practice. Soil moisture can increase from landscape watering, poor grading, and drainage and utility leaks, all of which are common occurrences and are hard to control. A decrease in soil moisture due to excessive evaporation and what's known as evapotranspiration is also hard to control and just as problematic.

Experience with thousands of homes with foundation distress problems provides the opportunity to see what mitigation methods work best for differing location, soil, and soil moisture conditions. Bob Brown has this experience. In addition to being an entrepreneur and inventor, he has developed numerous mitigation methods new to the industry, including releveling post-tensioned slabs and drying expansive soils with his patented AFS MoistureLevel System.

Historically a repair contractor would offer pier underpinning or grouting (or both) to mitigate a soil movement problem without any apparent consideration of the soil type or anticipated future soil movements. Bob Brown's approach includes assessing a foundation distress problem through a careful review that includes a site visit with damage assessment, floor-level (manometer) survey, and review and reporting that is sealed by a professional engineer. This process has been so successful that it is now being copied in part by foundation repair competitors.

Addressing a serious soil movement problem under a home can be less stressful for the homeowner if the soil problem is correctly identified and the roles of the repair contractor and engineering professionals are better understood. This book provides homeowners with important tools to better understand and navigate the mitigation of soil movement problems. Bob approaches these challenges from both an engineering and repair contracting perspective. He also dives into the repair contractor sales representative's interaction with the homeowner. This combination of experience and advice has been lacking in previous publications. A careful reading of this book will provide valuable insight into the ins and outs of the foundation repair industry as well as helpful tools to navigate mitigation measures necessary to reduce problems in homes founded over moisture-sensitive soils.

I recommend this book to both homeowners with soil movement problems and to professional engineers interested in better understanding the intricacies of soil movement distress mitigation.

—J. David Deatherage, PE
President, Copper State Engineering Inc.

INTRODUCTION

Figure 0.1

I started a business called Arizona Repair Masons in 1988 and another called Arizona Foundation Solutions in 2001, working for three decades in concrete leveling and underpinning. As my business increasingly focused on foundation repairs, I became devoted to this approach: *homeowners have the right to objective and accurate diagnoses and foundation repair recommendations based on real engineering principles.* You might ask, "What else could the job be based on?" Unfortunately, the answer is "meeting sales quotas."

I have felt a ton of pressure to sell underpinning to every customer. Pressure came from a variety of sources: suppliers looking for us to sell their products; our sales force and workers, who all depend on our revenue to earn a living; and my own concerns about having a profitable bottom line. It is frustrating to walk away from jobs and not sell any products or services to a customer who is pleading for relief after a house has sustained serious damage. I have done just that for many years. It takes a tremendous amount of expertise, honesty, and integrity to be forthright and not take advantage of the customer. I have prided myself and my company on these qualities since starting my business.

If you don't know what underpinning is, I'll briefly explain that and numerous other technical terms in the pages ahead—and again in a glossary at the front of the book—to help make you an informed consumer. But I won't skimp on technical details because this book has information that will be eye-opening even to the experts, and if you're not an expert, you deserve to know the technical details too.

Across America all foundation contractors face the same battle. Many lack the skills or the will to distinguish between two completely different types of building foundation damage: floor slab heave and footing settlement. As a result, many homeowners have been paying for repairs with little or no benefit—repairs that may actually be counterproductive.

I'm writing this book to help everyone learn the concepts and techniques for understanding the difference between heave and settlement. It will be up to the homeowners and contractors to use this information in an honest and productive way.

My Concrete Path to Business Success

Growing up in fairly humble circumstances, I was never an exceptional student. I struggled with dyslexia and attention deficit hyperactivity disorder (ADHD). But I had a strong level of persistence, a burning desire to succeed, and an independent streak that helps me engage in out-of-the-box thinking. Like many growing up in my generation, my first paid work was mowing lawns, which I started to do when the mower handles still reached almost over my head. I used to work for my father's employer, gluing pennies to mailers for sixty cents an hour. I worked harder and longer than most of my older siblings, and quite often they would come to me for loans, which I would provide at healthy interest rates.

My father lost all of his retirement nest egg building homes during the interest rate bubble of the late 1970s. Despite this setback, I was determined to get my college education. I didn't have much in savings, and I would need to drive to work and school. I borrowed a little money from a friend and went to an automobile auction, where I bought an old Chevy LUV pickup for six hundred dollars. When they started the engine, it raised a plume of smoke about thirty feet high. I figured I could replace the engine and still be in it for a decent price. As I drove home, I thought, "Instead of replacing the engine now, why don't I drive it until the engine goes and then replace it?" I drove that old truck for two years. I'd started working in concrete and masonry and would drive around to shopping centers, getting the property managers' names and offering to fix their curbs. I'd fill my pickup with bags of concrete that I would mix by hand in a wheelbarrow before getting to work replacing planter curbs.

The only way I could keep the old truck from overheating in the summertime was to drive with the heater on full blast when it already was 120 degrees in Phoenix. I suppose I've built up some sort of tolerance to heat, which is fortunate since my business is based in the Arizona desert.

My work was sweaty and dirty, but it enabled me to finally graduate from Arizona State University in 1984 with degrees in architecture and finance. I don't do concrete and masonry work anymore, but I still do other work for some of those early customers.

In the early years of running my business, I had lots of ups and downs. After a day's work, I would be sitting at a desk in my bedroom, still doing quotes and billings. I remember having a sports injury that required surgery on my ankle, after which I wasn't allowed to put any weight on the foot for twelve weeks. That left me hopping around job sites on one foot. In that era, I was mixing concrete in a wheelbarrow. I remember my jubilation when I finally saved up five hundred dollars to buy a used concrete mixer. Eventually I was also able to upgrade from a bedroom desk to a real office. It was in a house I paid for by also making it a one-bedroom rental.

Figures 0.2–0.7

TOP (L): Me in 2000 doing my first pile load test. (R): One of my imaginative contraptions—my own self-propelled concrete mixture.
MIDDLE (L): This is a picture of our first yard—a converted residential location. (R): The front of my first office and one-bedroom rental.
BOTTOM (L): Me on the left sharing a booth with Sunland Asphalt at an industry show. Eddie Basha once asked me, "Bob, why do you feel compelled to wear a tie with your Levi's?" (R): Me and two workers after a job in Flagstaff. It's a good thing I was wearing goggles!

Today we have over two million dollars' worth of specialized equipment and vehicles. We have a dedicated team that cares about our customers and three operating facilities that are wonderful but already too small for our growing business.

A "Mad Scientist" Approach to Problem Solving

Over the years I've tried to look at the needs of our community and provide a service that was not being met as well as it could have been. I have always believed that I need to understand the problem before trying to fix it. That sounds simple enough. But I have had more crazy inventions and ideas than I can remember while trying to think out of the box and solve problems. My employees call me the Dirt Whisperer and joke that I'm a mad scientist.

It is my transformative purpose in life to help homeowners recognize what they should expect from a proper foundation investigation. They have a right to objective and accurate diagnoses and recommendations based on real engineering principles as opposed to salesmanship.

It is my transformative purpose in life to help homeowners recognize what they should expect from a proper foundation investigation. They have a right to objective and accurate diagnoses and recommendations based on real engineering principles as opposed to salesmanship. It is also my purpose in life to bring to homeowners viable solutions for foundation heaving that are practical, affordable, and effective in dealing with this problem. I am licensing this technology to installers all across the United States. When I attended a conference in Texas that attracted installers from around the country, I shared details of my work and got an extremely positive response.

The biggest kick I get in my work life is taking a very perplexing and difficult problem and finding a solution that works and is cost effective. I am a naturally curious person, and I love to learn what I might be missing when faced with a problem. See my author's website (www.foundationrepairsecrets.com) for examples and deeper dives into many of these subjects.

Continuing education is important in my business. That's why I have included some of my certifications with my name on the cover of this book: the National Certified Foundation Repair Specialist (NCFRS) designation requires passing a rigorous exam to demonstrate mastery of that field. Passing the LEED AP exam shows proficiency in sustainable building design and construction. NRPP is the National Radon Proficiency Program, which indicates that one has the skill and expertise required to successfully complete testing and remediation of a naturally occurring radioactive gas that can cause cancer.

I am also Level 1 certified from the Post-Tensioning Institute and am Level 1 certified as a moisture-measurement specialist from the International Institute of Concrete Repair. These certifications may be reassuring to customers, but more importantly, the study involved has deepened my ability to help homeowners with problems that can be dangerous and costly.

Don't Gamble; It's Your Home!

The largest investments most people will ever make, of course, are in their homes. But even if that were not the case, why would anyone want to play smoke-and-mirror games with contractors in the place they live, raise a family, entertain their friends and relatives, spend the majority of their time—and now work?

When a house has foundation problems, action must be taken. Having people come in to diagnose the foundation problems is the logical first step. Think about the motivations, credentials, and science—if any—that will go into diagnosing. Can you trust them with the future of your home if they might have a vested interest in steering you in one direction or another to fit what they have to offer you? To see how this distressing scenario could happen, read on.

In the pages ahead, I'll start by introducing the technical experts who reviewed and can vouch for the innovative methods I am employing in my work and detailing in this book. Chapter 1 is a primer on foundations and their vulnerabilities, which are rooted primarily in the soil forces explained in chapter 2. Then we will dig deep into what happens when a homeowner calls a foundation repair contractor for help. The middle chapters explain the detective work and research that should go into a proper diagnosis of the problem. Homeowners will learn the many questions they can ask to ensure they are being offered an appropriate solution.

I already have made clear that this book contains strong opinions about whether the industry generally gives homeowners the kind of expert investigations they deserve. I am not just showing that many repairs are useless or detrimental, but I am also offering a smarter approach for a common foundation repair. The last one-third of the book reveals best practices for how, why, and when to remediate a heaved slab because contractors should be on the level.

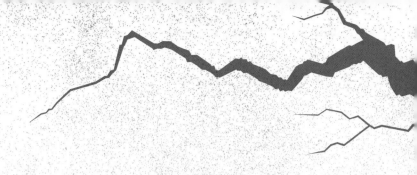

TECHNICAL EXPERTS

Meet some of the experts who supported our successful patent application for the MoistureLevel® System discussed in chapter 8. These engineers have supported the development of the system with advice and technical direction. The PE designation after their names means they are licensed professional engineers who have passed intensive competency exams after getting their four-year college degrees and working under a professional engineer for at least four years. To retain their state licenses, PEs must continually maintain and improve their skills throughout their careers.

Figures 0.8 and 0.9

J. David Deatherage, PE

PRESIDENT, COPPER STATE ENGINEERING

Mr. Deatherage is a senior geotechnical engineer specializing in soils and foundation investigations whose experience includes design and construction engineering on more than forty flood control and mining-related dam projects. Most of Mr. Deatherage's work is in Arizona, though his team has worked in Jamaica, Peru, and Mexico on several dam- and mining-related projects. Specialties include investigating expansive and collapsible soils, performing design and construction engineering for dams and copper mining heap leach facilities, and completing forensic investigations for geotechnical-related failures.

Claudia Zapata, PhD, PE

ASSOCIATE PROFESSOR, ARIZONA STATE UNIVERSITY

Dr. Zapata was appointed assistant professor in the Department of Civil and Environmental Engineering at Arizona State University in 2006. She received her PhD in geoenvironmental engineering from ASU in 1999. Dr. Zapata's primary research area is unsaturated soil behavior, focusing on fluid flow and volume-change modeling for expansive soils, with applications related to the behavior of pavement subgrades and slabs-on-grade foundation design. Specialties include pavement performance due to environmental factors as well as the fluid flow and volume-change properties of expansive soils under slabs-on-grade residential foundations.

CHAPTER 1

A PRACTICAL GUIDE TO UNDERSTANDING YOUR FOUNDATION

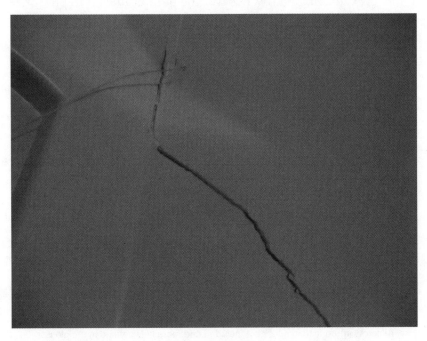

Figure 1.1

One of the worst foundation disasters I ever saw happened at a really nice modern home in North Scottsdale, a Phoenix suburb dotted with swimming pools where homes can sell for seven or eight figures. The problem was *settlement*.[1] It's common knowledge that a building can settle, and when floors are no longer level, tile, ceilings, and walls can crack. With an inch or two of settlement, windows and doors no longer operate smoothly. Most people probably associate these issues with old houses built prior to contemporary building codes. Or maybe someone who was not a professional home builder put up a summer cabin without permits and with the help of buddies whose only pay was the beer they consumed on the job. Often, though, the cause lies underground in changes occurring in one or more layers of soil.

In North Scottsdale, the issue was more unusual. The plumbing that pumped water into the nice swimming pool had a joint that somehow came unglued. Whenever the pump came on to pressurize the pool intake, the elbow popped off and injected water into the soil between the house and the pool. The house was built on gravelly, sandy, decomposed granite soil that just collapsed under those wet conditions. Soon the house had settled an astounding twelve inches. By the time I was called to the scene, ugly cracks had appeared in the exterior's painted stucco, and they were crudely patched. I think my company could have saved the house because we had successfully handled even more severe settlement. One time we dealt with settlement at a country club that had to be raised up twenty-four inches. But the North Scottsdale home was unfortunately declared a total loss and eventually was torn down after the couple divorced.

Understanding the nature and cause of a foundation problem is

---

1   All terms introduced in italics are included and more fully defined in the glossary at the beginning of the book.

the first step in determining how—or whether—it can be repaired. To provide a sense of the different types of foundation systems, we will begin by explaining three common ones that I regularly encounter. Before we can discuss foundation problems and potential solutions for homeowners, we need to understand how foundations are built, how they interact with the soils, and how this interaction affects the super-structure of the house components. We will explore the mysteries of soil, how soil varies in different regions and climates, and how soil interacts with each of the foundation types.

I had a friend once tell me that all roads are dirt roads. It doesn't matter whether you paint the surface with asphalt or concrete or whether you slap on a slurry seal or go green and rubberize the pavement with recycled tires—the road is still supported and made primarily of dirt! The foundations of homes and other buildings work the same way. They are all supported by the soil underneath—or they are supposed to be.

I'm going to provide examples based on my firsthand experience in Arizona. We have similar soil conditions in parts of California, Nevada, New Mexico, Oregon, eastern Washington, and generally west of the Mississippi. Other places may have different soils, but we'll discuss how the basic concepts still apply, even though the soils will sometimes interact differently with the foundation.

To help explain how these systems work, we will include some basic background about the materials that go into a home's foundation and what can make it vulnerable to structural damage.

Typical Conventional Foundation with a Floating Slab

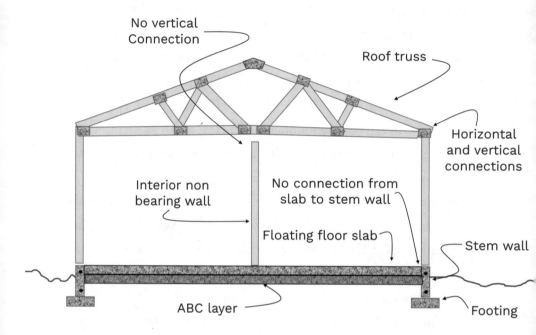

Figure 1.2: This drawing represents the typical foundation found throughout much of the Southwest. This was predominantly the way most contractors built in warmer climates prior to 2003. The ABC layer refers to the sand and gravel used in some places as a transition between the soil and the concrete slab. You can also see cold joints here, which occurs when an area joins two portions of concrete that were placed at different times. This means the joint has no continuous integrity and can easily move separately.

In this conventional foundation with trusses, the perimeter supports all of the roof load, which is distributed via the roof truss system. Some components you see are

- the *footing*, which lies in the soil, typically eighteen to thirty-six inches below grade to provide support for loads above it;

- the *stem wall*, which sits on top of the footing to support the frame or masonry wall above it; and

- the *floor slab*, which is the concrete placed in the floor of a house.

In conventional foundations, the interior floor slab is not a part of the foundation system. It is a "floating floor slab" not physically connected to the stem walls. The gap between the interior non-load-bearing walls and the trusses ensures that roof loads do not put weight on interior walls.

Concrete, invented by the ancient Romans, is a common form of pavement made up of sand, rocks, cement, and water. When combined, a chemical reaction occurs and transforms those ingredients into a solid material. The *cement* is made from limestone—a plentiful rock thanks to all of the lobsters and other crustaceans whose remains are calcified by the oceans—transformed by extreme heat and ground to a fine powder. More than two thousand years ago, the Romans got calcified lime to make concrete by mining ashes deposited by the volcanic eruption of Mount Vesuvius near Pozzuoli, Italy. In construction today, *pozzolana* refers to naturally reactive materials used to strengthen concrete. Both sand and cement can comprise a variety of inorganic and organic materials, so concrete is a building material with endless variations.

As strong and reliable as concrete is, we'll see that it has vulnerabilities, often involving what's supporting it. In the context of this book, *heave* refers

Both sand and cement can comprise a variety of inorganic and organic materials, so concrete is a building material with endless variations.

to how certain types of soil swell when they get wet. The expansion usually occurs in an upward motion, and that can damage a concrete slab. *Spread footings* surround the typical conventional foundation; they are adjacent to the slab but are not holding it down. They are not attached. If the slab heaves, the footings can heave with it, but more often they do not. Conversely, if the footings settle, the slab usually does also. The weight then would no longer be spread evenly along the footings, which could lead to cracks in perimeter walls.

Typical Post-Tensioned Foundation in the Southwest

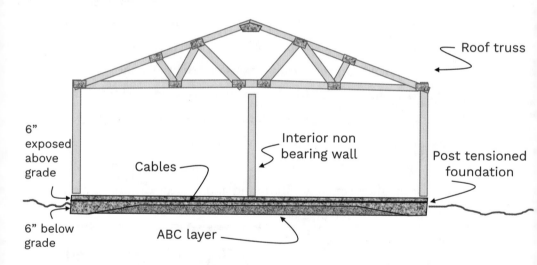

Figure 1.3: Around 2003, most builders in Arizona and areas with similar soil started transitioning to this type of foundation system.

At the beginning of the twenty-first century, some engineers and contractors got together and decided that they wanted to improve the standard foundation systems. Their approach—reinforcing concrete with strong steel tendons—caught on and has been heavily promoted by a national trade association called the Post-Tensioning Institute. That organization sets standards and provides certifications. Because foundations react differently to diverse soil forces, there are regional variations in the post-tensioned foundations. Instead of parallel tendons reinforcing the concrete, which create a slab of uniform thickness, it's common in Texas to see tendons that are layered top to bottom, reminiscent of a waffle pattern.

As with most conventional systems, the trusses distribute all of the weight to the perimeter of a post-tensioned foundation. The black line through the concrete in the drawing represents a series of cables in both directions that are tightened after the concrete is poured.

Different materials have different strengths and weaknesses. For example, metal rods can be easy to bend but hard to break. Glass is durable but can crack. In a *post-tensioned slab*, steel cables are tensioned, or pulled tight, after the concrete slab is poured in place. The tightening of the cables puts the concrete in *compression* to strengthen its ability to bear weight. The cables are great in tension, so they also compensate for the weak tensile strength of concrete. Tensile strength is the ability to hold together when being pulled apart.

> Many homeowners think that because they have post-tensioned foundations, they are safe from foundation problems. However, that is simply not true. We have repaired many homes with post-tensioned foundation problems. Some of these systems are designed to operate under ideal conditions and don't function as well when those conditions are not ideal.

This system has weaknesses: there is very little edge protection to stop water from getting underneath the slab, making it very vulnerable to heave, which tends to damage interior and exterior walls.

Typical Crawl Space for Pier-and-Beam Foundation

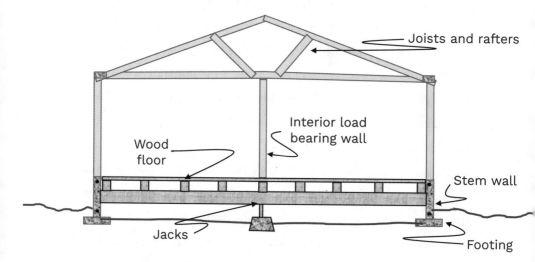

Figure 1.4: This is the typical system that was used prior to about the 1960s and in cooler climates.

A lot of houses, including ones you might see in a historic district, have several steps leading up to a porch, indicating that the house is elevated. Depending on the region, crawl space foundations may be sitting on piers, which are sunk into the ground, or on aboveground piers that sit on footings.

A pier-and-beam foundation elevated twelve to twenty-four inches or more would allow access underneath. In colder climates, it's not uncommon to have a larger crawl space between the main floor and the dirt below. But in Phoenix I have seen crawl spaces a scant twelve inches off the ground that were impossible to get into for a foundation repair. A house on a hill might have a deeper crawl space on one side than another.

I have crawled under homes and asked myself, "What's holding this thing up?" It's scary! The adventure begins when a customer calls about a problem in one part of the house and wants to have just that section fixed. But an engineer takes a look and can see that none of the house is structurally sound. My job is to reconcile what the customer wants with the reality that the engineer is afraid of being held accountable for future problems that won't be prevented by a limited repair.

In the older variations of this foundation type, there typically is no truss system above; therefore, some of the walls on the interior help carry the roof loads. Since trusses were employed in the mid-1960s, they are not found in historic homes with crawl spaces. Besides the footings on the perimeter, there are interior jacks to support the floor from underneath. If the house was built in a time or place where builders didn't have to meet modern building codes, the vertical supports might be placed irregularly. Or worse, someone might have cut some wooden logs and stood them on end as supports, but now they are leaning precariously.

A pier-and-beam foundation is less vulnerable to heave than the newer system because it has no concrete floor slab for moisture to accumulate underneath (as will be explained later). Heave is still possible, however, if there's a concrete slab for an adjacent garage. As in the newer foundation types, the pier-and-beam system interacts with the soil underneath, and the footings should be designed to resist settlement. In parts of Texas or Louisiana, often the piers are basically round concrete columns that go deep into the soil and are used to support walls and columns. In other areas, stem walls above the footings might be made up of cinder blocks filled with concrete and reinforced with rebar.

Foundation contractors tend to call the vertical supports that hold up an above-grade span *piers*, even if *piles* would be more specific and technically correct. Variations in soil, climate, and building techniques dictate that piles come in a variety of shapes and sizes. They can be screwed or pushed into the ground, or both hammered and screwed, or concrete can be poured and set in predrilled holes. Terminology has regional variations. When relevant, this book will specify and describe types of piers, including piles and caissons.

Climate and Other Considerations

Climate and other geographic variations play a major role in determining what foundation systems are used around the world. In the northern United States, for example, it makes sense to dig below the frost level and install building systems in basements. Texas is an epicenter of foundation problems because its soil has really expansive *clay soil* that goes through wet and dry weather cycles. The seasonal variations lead to shrinking and swelling of those clays, producing all kinds of stress on foundations. Arizona, where I mostly work, has a desert climate where the soil has been dry for tens of thousands of years, but occasionally we have epic downpours. When you put a house on top of the desert soil, the roof will shed rain that will soak into the ground. Housing density affects whether that water has room to disperse. Imagine what happens when water gushes from a downspout into a really narrow side yard.

Compare that situation to a house on a lot in Texas where the soil has been wet for tens of thousands of years. Although that house will also shed rain, there's a danger the soil along the side of the house gradually may get drier than the soil under the house, creating a shrinkage danger on the foundation's perimeter. Soakers around the house can even out the moisture in the soil. Toward the end of this book, we'll discuss another approach that involves importing under the foundation the air that the soil is used to.

No matter what the climate is, or how the foundation is designed to support a building, a house still sits on soil. In the next chapter we'll focus on the dynamics of soil.

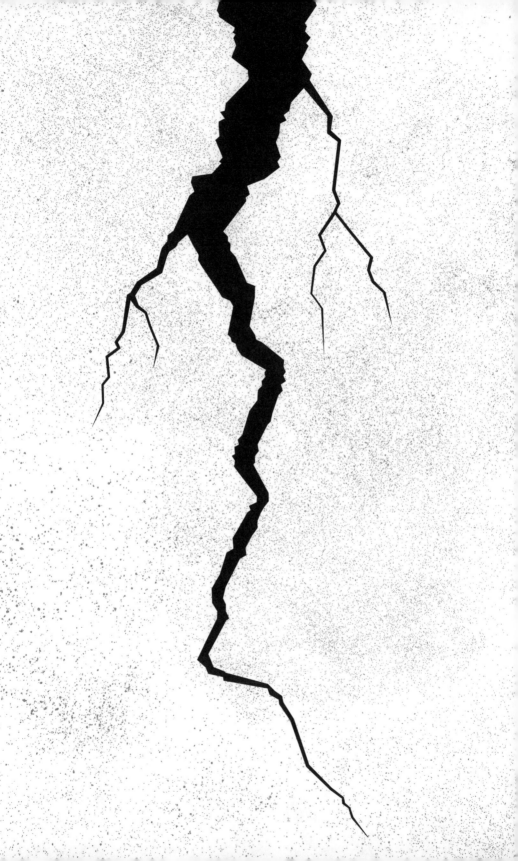

CHAPTER 2

SOIL DISCUSSION—HEAVE VERSUS SETTLEMENT

About ninety miles east of Phoenix is a historic small town called Globe that owes its existence to mining, mostly for copper. People in Globe have been pushing dirt around since prospectors found silver there in 1875. Digging and filling over many years resulted in the ground being much different from the compacted layers found in undisturbed soil. Somebody dumped dirt and who knows what other foreign objects into a big canyon and built a house on it, and when its foundation settled about twelve inches, the homeowners called me.

The situation I encountered in Globe is an extreme example of the reality that keeps me in business because it underlies all foundations, no matter what type: the soils under every home are different. Not only is each situation different, but each has layers that get deposited over millions or billions of years with different chemical composition, density, water content, and particle sizes. Soils consist of clays, sands or silts, gravel, and rock. Each of these components has various mineral makeup and compositions that we won't go into here beyond providing the big picture.

Let's Get Dirty

Figure 2.1

Most people picture settlement with these kinds of telltale signs of cracks forming in walls.

When land lots are developed, the builder *cuts* and *fills* the highs and lows to provide the levels needed to build houses, streets, and neighborhoods, often overcompacting them. As a result, some of those various layers end up closer to the surface than others because the layers are not flat, uniform, or level. Each of them conducts water differently and reacts to water differently. The result is a dynamic, constantly changing soil system at each location that is almost always in flux. It's like a seven-layer chip dip where each of the layers is always changing.

Many custom homes are not built using information from a geotechnical investigation to aid the designer in accommodating the complexity of soil variation, and many tract homes are built with sparse information at best. If a structure is built over *collapsible soil*—sands or silts that do not get consolidated well enough, water infiltrates into that soil. Sands or silts typically consolidate with additional moisture, and the load of a house pressing on top of the soil leads to settlement. If a structure is built over clay soils that dry out, the clays shrink, and the house also settles. This common problem occurs in most houses, especially in climates that are wetter. The soil has been wet for years, and when you put a structure on top—blocking rain or melting snow—it tends to dry out the soil underneath. It is even worse when there are droughts.

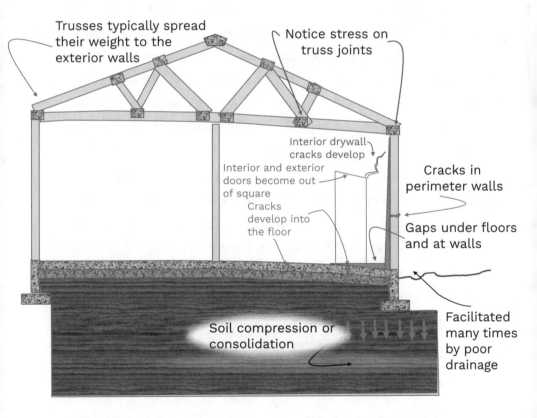

Figure 2.2: Soil compression or consolidation leads to settlement and cracks.

Understanding the cause of a foundation problem requires diagnosing how the soil is behaving. Let's start by examining how clay behaves versus the way sands and silts behave.

Clay particles typically are smaller by orders of magnitude than sand, so tiny that they require a scanning tunneling microscope to look at. Clay particles also typically have an affinity for water because they are negatively charged ions, which means that they have suction, and they pull water, which is a positively charged ion, toward them. They are like sponges, which expand when they get wet and shrink when they dry out. In the previous chapter, we discussed heave, in which certain types of soil swell when they get wet, damaging a concrete slab and interior walls. Expansive clays can cause heave. Expansive soils are defined as having a 2 percent swell or more upon wetting. It's possible that a house is built on top of clays that become supersaturated and then collapse, causing settlement. This phenomenon calls to mind the spectacular mudslides that occasionally topple a house on the West Coast, but normally this type of settlement is fairly rare and usually minor.

To put it simply, soil under a concrete slab might be either too dry or too wet. Either condition could lead to settlement. But depending on the soil, moisture accumulation could produce settlement or heave. The chapters ahead will discuss what homeowners should expect foundation contractors to do in response to these varying conditions. Homeowners can start by educating themselves with this brief guide to why moisture accumulates under a slab more so in drier climates and does not dissipate over time.

Four Mechanisms of Moisture Accumulation

1. SUCTION

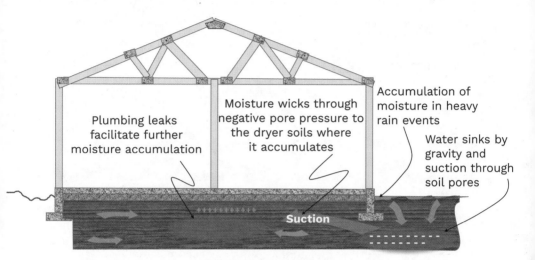

Plumbing leaks facilitate further moisture accumulation

Moisture wicks through negative pore pressure to the dryer soils where it accumulates

Accumulation of moisture in heavy rain events

Water sinks by gravity and suction through soil pores

Suction

Figure 2.3: Suction

Clay soil has a negative ionic charge. Water has a positive one. As a result, they are attracted to each other. *Geotechnical* engineers refer to this as negative pore pressure, but we can simply call it suction. Clay literally sucks!

Although water moves very slowly through some clays at about three inches per year, the horizontal layers in which the soil is deposited allow for somewhat faster movement. During heavy rain, overwa-

Even if the sun comes out and dries the soil where it was initially soaking wet, it will not dry it enough to reverse suction. Each rain event has a cumulative effect.

tering, air-conditioning condensate drips, etc., with typically poor drainage, water soaks down to the soil below, and because the soil in the center of the slab is much drier, water is attracted to it. Even if the sun comes out and dries the soil where it was initially soaking wet, it will not dry it enough to reverse suction. Each rain event has a cumulative effect.

2. TEMPERATURE

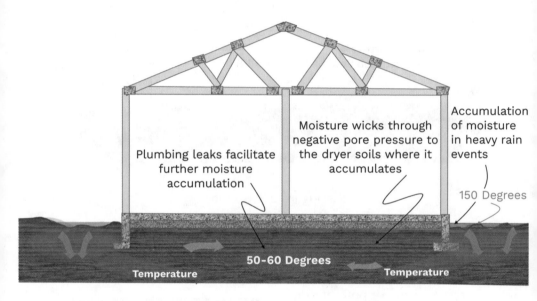

Figure 2.4: Temperature

With the inside of the house air-conditioned, the soil under the slab in the center areas can be much cooler than the soil around the house, particularly as the sun beats down on it. In areas like Phoenix, where my business is based, the differential can be as much as eighty degrees. A professor of geotechnical engineering at Arizona State University, Dr. Claudia Zapata, has conducted several studies documenting the effects of water migrating to cooler soils.

3. THE STACK EFFECT

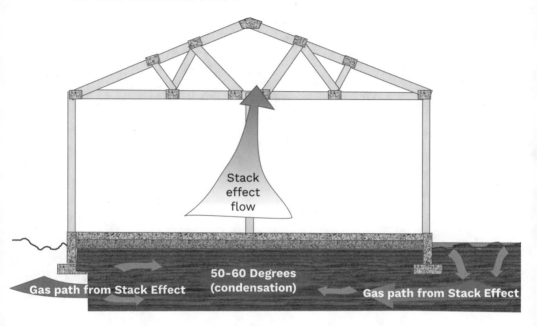

Figure 2.5: Stack effect

Radon scientists have documented the stack effect for many years. As hot air rises to the attic and exits the vents, it is replaced with air and gases from the lower portions of the structure, particularly through the foundation from the soil under it and around it. The stack effect has been documented to pull radon, a radioactive gas, into the structure from as far away as twenty feet from the house's perimeter.

Water vapor is a gas as well and follows the same path, except that as water reaches the cooler interior soils, it cools and condenses to a liquid. As it does so, it develops surface tension and much less molecular energy for diffusion. Thus, it is unable to likely follow other gases into the interior of the home, but much of it is trapped under the slab, where it accumulates.

4. THORNTHWAITE EFFECT

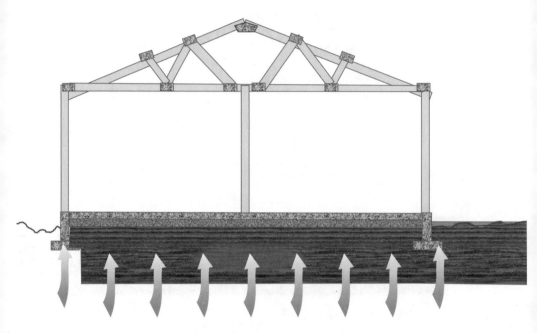

Figure 2.6: Evapotranspertive cycle

Vapor rises up from the water table or any other underground water sources in a process called *evapotranspiration*. This process is a complicated geotechnical concept, but it can be easily demonstrated wherever plastic is buried in the ground and water accumulates underneath.

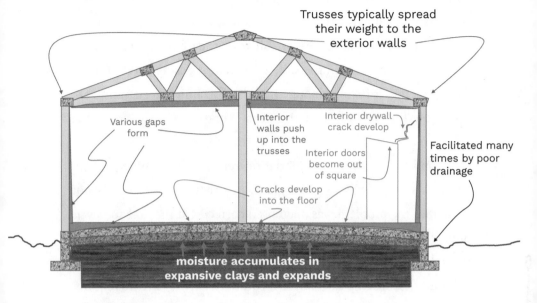

Figure 2.7: The result of these four mechanisms is the accumulation of water where it wets expansive clay soil, resulting in upward heave.

Who Studies This Stuff?

All kinds of engineers work in the construction industry, but those in one particular branch, geotechnical engineers, study the soil issues discussed in this chapter. Depending upon state regulations, someone studying civil engineering in college might have to declare the geotechnical specialty while still in school and pass exams after graduation. A structural engineer may be an expert in the foundation systems and aboveground portions of construction but not qualified to write a report about soil conditions.

Geotechnical engineers are commonly employed in commercial new construction, but note that many of them work regularly in forensics—investigating what's gone wrong. An investigation could involve looking at aerial photographs of a site, but geotechnical engineers typically visit the site, drill holes, take samples, and write reports explaining the results of soil tests they have performed. If there are contaminants in the soil, a different specialty, environmental engineering, is involved. State boards of technical registration are responsible for ensuring that engineers work only in the areas that they are trained and competent to practice in.

A building permit for foundation repair work may require an engineer's stamp approving the plans, but that regulation does not ensure that the problem was diagnosed correctly. If the diagnosis was done by a salesperson or contractor, you may have no assurance that the problem was correctly diagnosed and it may not perform well over time. The spacing calculations required by cities have no requirement of diagnosing and recommending solutions for any particular problem.

Expertise matters when investigating a foundation problem. Some individuals claim that floor slab heave will dissipate if left alone and eventually take care of itself. This is not only false, but in fact, moisture will continue to accumulate in arid climates over time by the four methods we explained in this chapter. In my experience, sales personnel can make some pretty outrageous claims and are usually not held accountable by any governing ethics board. The next chapter explains what often goes wrong when a homeowner seeks expert help with a foundation problem.

CHAPTER 3

THE DIRTY LITTLE SECRET OF THE FOUNDATION REPAIR INDUSTRY

A couple I'll call the Diamonds wanted to remodel their home with new tile flooring. Since the existing flooring had a lot of cracks, they were worried the new tile would also crack, and they asked us and a competitor to examine the house. We did a complete report, with our engineer's recommendations for a MoistureLevel System® to control the moisture level under the house. The competitor sent out a nonengineer who convinced the Diamonds that improving the gutters and drainage around the house would solve their problems.

Our engineer clearly spelled out in their opinion that drying out only the perimeter with better drainage would not solve the problem of moisture buildup under the center portions of the home and could actually make the cracking worse. I shouldn't really blame the homeowners for taking the wrong advice because these sales guys are trained to project confidence and come off as wizards who fully understand what's going on and are deeply motivated with a vested interest. But ironically the Diamonds hired us to perform the work recommended by the competitor on the gutters and drainage and to stitch the cracks in the foundation, which we did.

A year later, the new tile cracked, and the Diamonds filed a complaint with the Arizona Registrar of Contractors blaming us. In a follow-up meeting with the customer, I asked, "Why didn't you follow the engineer's recommendations?" The Diamonds responded that "the sales guy from the other company told us we didn't need that." Why did they believe him? "Well, the engineers at your company, they work for you, so all they're trying to do is get lots of work for your company." In fact, most state laws and engineering association ethics boards prohibit engineers from getting paid anything other than a salary or on an hourly or per-project basis. They cannot receive compensation based on the outcome of a job, like a salesperson earning a commission.

Closing a Sale on One Visit

Taking a commissioned salesperson's uneducated advice makes no sense to me, but it is often what happens when a typical homeowner calls a foundation repair contractor just about anywhere in North America. The contractor sends out a salesperson to the home to do a "one-call close." This consists of meeting and interviewing the homeowner, examining the home, drawing up a floor plan, taking some elevation readings, maybe taking a few photos, figuring out on the spot what the problem is, and recommending a solution. Drawing up the "repair plan" and contract and taking the down payment all may happen in just one visit. No second opinions are solicited, not even an informal review by the boss or a colleague back in the office.

See chapter 5 for a taste of what it really takes to do a proper investigation—you will soon agree it cannot be done on the spot in one visit if it is to be done properly.

There are many problems with this approach. We will go through them one at a time.

1. SALESPEOPLE'S LACK OF FORMAL EDUCATION

I know of few foundation repair salespeople who have a clear, documented formal education in structural and geotechnical engineering. They can make lots of claims like "I have been trained by my supplier." Or they might say, "I have been doing this for thirty-five years and have been educated in the school of hard knocks." As the previous chapter showed, soil mechanics is a complicated field with easily misunderstood effects. That's why the requirements to become an engineer are so rigorous.

Foundation salespeople are needed in the industry and do play an important role, as we will explain later. But the industry has put an unfair burden on the consumer to recognize this gap in qualifications.

 Soil mechanics is a complicated field with easily misunderstood effects. That's why the requirements to become an engineer are so rigorous.

Engineers

- Four to five years of university training followed by three years of apprenticeship and passing two very difficult exams.

- Held accountable by the state boards of technical registration.

- Impartial, objective, and unbiased.

- Follow engineering investigative procedures standardized by professional consensus.

- Utilize peer review and multiple opinions.

- Gauge severity on numerical, objective criteria, using allowable margins set by consensus.

- Have many more resources at their disposal.

Salespeople

- Most receive a few days training from a single-product supplier.

- No third party holding them or the company accountable for their statements.

- Typically paid based on products sold.

- Follow diagnosis training taught to them by their product supplier.

- Usually perform their work on the spot while at the home.

- Many come from out of state and are clueless about local geology, building practices, and other important factors.

2. TRAINING FROM SUPPLIERS

While most foundation repair salespeople get some training from suppliers on how to conduct an investigation, I have never seen a recognized standard being taught. For example, when gauging how bad the settlement is, I have seen some sales guys use builders' levels, and others use zip levels; some roll golf balls around. I have even heard of one who says he takes off his shoes and "feels what the problem is." Forensic engineers do have recognized standards, such as the Post-

Tensioning Institute (PTI) guide, or the Foundation Performance Association (FPA) standards. The foundation repair industry largely ignores these standards, either because its people have not heard of them or consider them too rigorous.

3. CONFLICTS OF INTEREST

Having the same person determine what is wrong, which parts are bad enough to fix, and how to fix them and then collecting a sales commission for the work that's done is an inherent conflict of interest. Sometimes these salespeople are good at reading people and tell homeowners whatever they want to hear. That approach creates good feelings but is neither scientific nor objective.

4. MYOPIC SOLUTIONS

Foundation repair contractors typically provide one solution for foundation problems: *push piles or helical piles.* Chapter 7 has more information about these systems, in which steel piles are basically screwed or pushed into the ground to provide foundational support. These are good products and generally perform well. However, they provide a solution for only one problem: settlement. If the problem is something else, they have nothing to offer—sort of like a one-trick pony. To paraphrase Abraham Maslow, author of *The Psychology of Science*, "If the only tool you have is a hammer, then all your problems start looking like nails." Suppliers train contractors to recognize settlement and sell piles. If the problem is outside of that, the salesmen are largely ignorant of what's going on. Sometimes foundation contractors can sub out grading and drainage, but that work is not typically where they make significant money. Is it a coincidence they are not often recommending such work?

5. INATTENTION TO DETAILS

The next three chapters will show just how rigorous foundation inspections should be when they follow the steps recommended in the engineering guidelines. These investigations require very detailed work by someone with a detail-oriented personality. Salespeople have a lot of talents (most of our homeowners love our salespeople), but being detail oriented is usually not among them. It's like asking a salesperson to do bookkeeping work. They might muddle through it, but it's not where they shine.

6. DONE ON SITE IN ONE VISIT

In my opinion, a rigorous investigation cannot be done on site, on the spot while at the home. I have asked every engineer I encounter if they would document the site, perform an investigation, analyze the results, come to conclusions, make recommendations, develop a repair plan, and document it all on site in one visit. I have talked with hundreds of engineers, and none have said they would do it. Yet foundation salespeople, who have substantially less expertise, are expected to complete this impossible task every time. Human nature guarantees they will succumb to biases in that situation.

7. LACK OF OVERSIGHT

Engineering standards require an engineer to vouch for initial reports not just by signing them but also by affixing a seal. For this formal stamp of approval, the on-site data-gathering technician must work under the direct supervision of the engineer of record for the project. Most foundation repair contractors have no in-house engineer, making this direct supervision impossible. Sealed reports are not common because the sales practice of completing all the tasks in one visit is incompatible with the engineers' culture of oversight and peer review.

8. DIFFERENT SKILL SETS

Salespeople have valuable skills, just not typically engineering-type skills. Engineers, on the other hand, often come up short in the skills required in communicating, advising, and counseling consumers. See the comparison chart below.

Engineers

- Detailed observation

- Abstract thought

- Mathematical thinking

- Precision

- Hypothesizing

- Analyzing data

- Data-driven decision-making

- Objectivity

Salespeople

- Listening

- Teaching

- Understanding goals

- Identifying concerns

- Communicating

- Guiding

- Advising

- Counseling

- Multitasking

9. INSUFFICIENT DATA

The symptoms of settlement and heave are very close and often confused, as the next few chapters will make clearer. Standing in a single room, it is nearly impossible to be sure which condition is occurring. Without getting additional viewpoints and analyzing all of the available and often contradictory data carefully, it is very easy to mix up heave and settlement. And the solutions are very different.

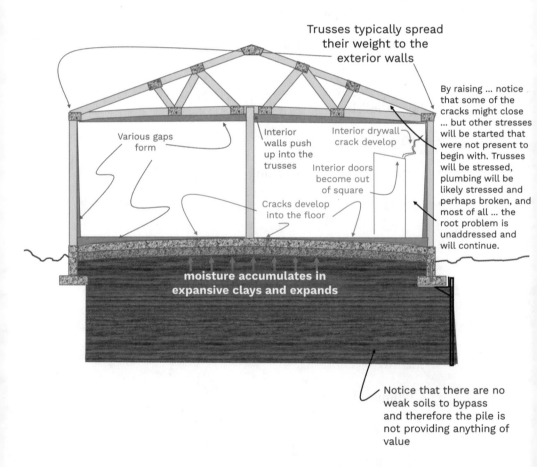

Trusses typically spread their weight to the exterior walls

Various gaps form

Interior walls push up into the trusses

Interior drywall crack develop

Interior doors become out of square

Cracks develop into the floor

By raising ... notice that some of the cracks might close ... but other stresses will be started that were not present to begin with. Trusses will be stressed, plumbing will be likely stressed and perhaps broken, and most of all ... the root problem is unaddressed and will continue.

moisture accumulates in expansive clays and expands

Notice that there are no weak soils to bypass and therefore the pile is not providing anything of value

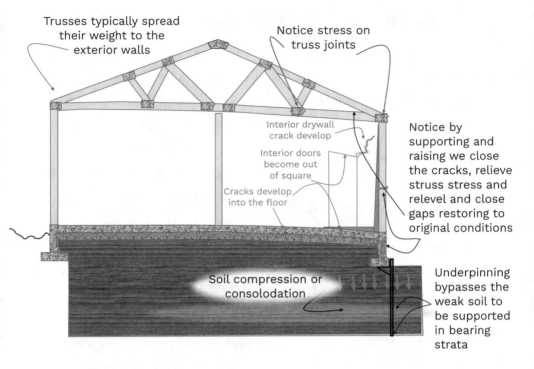

Trusses typically spread their weight to the exterior walls

Notice stress on truss joints

Interior drywall crack develop

Interior doors become out of square

Cracks develop into the floor

Notice by supporting and raising we close the cracks, relieve struss stress and relevel and close gaps restoring to original conditions

Soil compression or consolodation

Underpinning bypasses the weak soil to be supported in bearing strata

Figures 3.1 and 3.2: The cutaway (section view) of the house on the left demonstrates center heave, while the one on the right demonstrates edge settlement. By standing in a single room, one can see that in both cases, the signs of stress are so similar that it is almost impossible to tell them apart just by looking at them.

10. MOTIVATIONAL ISSUES

Often a foundation repair contractor has nothing to offer for heave but does have a solution to sell for settlement. If a thorough investigation determines the problem is caused entirely by heave, the contractor can go home hungry or perhaps offer the customer a nonsolution of grading and drainage. The contractor's rationale often will go something like this: "Well, there may be some heave, but it could be settlement also, so let's just put some piles in to be sure."

Avoiding Being Hoodwinked

Consumers cannot be expected to be foundation experts. For their own protection, homeowners always should do a few simple things: ask important questions (listed in chapter 6), demand that contractors follow industry standards, and hold them accountable by always getting results of an inspection or investigation with written observations and recommendations.

 Ask important questions (listed in chapter 6), demand that contractors follow industry standards, and hold them accountable by always getting results of an inspection or investigation with written observations and recommendations.

Pros and Cons of Design/Build

I had lunch the other day with a prominent structural engineer in the Phoenix area. Our discussion was wide ranging, covering many topics. Some topics that we discussed were the pros and cons of in-house engineering for foundation repairs.

The cons of in-house engineering include, among other things, the perception of a lack of objectivity. Since the engineers work for a foundation repair company, their advice could be seen as biased. Perhaps the culture or company structure theoretically could influence an engineer to lean toward recommending repairs more than usual, especially if the corporate structure has the engineer under the direct supervision of someone in sales or marketing. I doubt any good forensic engineer would agree to having a marketing or sales supervisor, but I suppose it is theoretically possible. We certainly would never agree to such a corporate structure and, in fact, value the independence of our engineering team.

I wonder in fact how this really differs from engineers who receive 95 percent of their revenues from home builders. If those same engineers are doing forensic investigations on behalf of those same home builders when unhappy homeowners reach out to the home builders with complaints, could the corporate structure and culture contribute to making recommendations favorable to their home builder clients?

Naturally the homeowner's best choice might be to find an independent engineer who does not receive the majority of their income from either foundation repair contractors or from homebuilders. That could be a tall order, considering this is mostly a geotechnical problem that tries to understand serviceability reactions of a structure to soil movements. Logically, geotechnical engineers are better suited in some ways than structural engineers, but there are some structural aspects, so it really requires both. Our experience has shown that geotechs are better at writing reports than drawing and detailing plans, whereas structurals are less experienced in writing reports. So in the end, there are not many good choices for independent engineers who are helpful and truly independent for homeowners, for foundation repairs have both geotechnical and structural capabilities. Perhaps that may change someday.

One strong pro for in-house engineering for foundation repair is single-source accountability. If the plans for the repair come from one source and the actual work comes from another, then when things don't perform, it can be difficult to determine who is at fault. Both parties naturally will point to each other rather than themselves in the case of a dispute, leaving the homeowner with no clear responsible party. This can be avoided when the engineer and contractor are both working for the same company. With this type of arrangement, the homeowner has a much simpler action when trying to understand who is responsible for performance.

The best possible choice for homeowners is an engineering practice that is both structural and geotechnical and not associated with either a repair contractor or a home builder. Until such a practice exists, we find the most practical and cost-effective solution is for a design/build practice with both structurals and geotechs that operate independently from sales and marketing.

In this chapter, I have taken a critical look at standard operating procedures in an industry that I have worked in for many years. The realization that these practices were obscuring rather than curing the problem of heave—and sometimes worsening it—dawned on me gradually over time. At first, I could not put a finger on what exactly the problem with the process was. I knew that if the salesperson wanted to, they could take advantage of the homeowner to boost their commission. I caught one of my sales guys doing it in my early days in my company and put a stop to it. Then I remember going to lunch with local engineers and asking a lot of questions about how to determine the difference between settlement and heave. The more information I picked up, the more I understood how it was a lot more complicated than my fellow contractors and I had assumed it to be.

Sometimes there is no "smoking gun," with an easily identified solution, and sometimes the problems may be masked by something other than soil-caused issues. Later we will discuss the levels of investigations and their requirements ... some being to fix a problem, others to discover causal mechanisms or see whether there are parties at fault.

The next chapter explains this complexity and all of the factors involved in investigating a foundation problem.

CHAPTER 4

WHAT A REAL FOUNDATION INVESTIGATION INVOLVES

An elderly widow living in a retirement community east of Phoenix called in to a local radio show whose host dispenses home-spun home improvement advice. She had a foundation problem, and one of our competitors proposed a repair plan that would cost more than $165,000, which was almost as much as her tract house was worth at the time.

"I can't afford that. What am I going to do?" the widow asked the host.

This happened about fifteen years ago, but I remember it for a few reasons. It was a classic case of a repair contractor not knowing about heave and moisture control and proposing *underpinning* and *compaction grouting* all around the perimeter of the house that would not solve the problem. Underpinning is the process of driving piles down through the soil layers until they meet strong resistance. It's like putting the house on stilts so it can be releveled. Compaction grouting is a technique that can fill sinkholes or level sinking foundations by injecting a cementlike substance into the ground to fill voids. That process may sound simple, but technology and expertise are required to best determine where to drill, how deep, and how much grouting gets piped in.

The host knew about types of reports that we did, which were then called manometers after a measuring instrument we were using. In a little mix-up on air, the host seemed to be advising this widow that a contractor could come out and give her a mammogram! We didn't do that, of course, but we did come out and diagnose the foundation problem.

When we performed our investigation, the data pointed strongly to one corner of the home that clearly needed underpinning, which we were able to do for about $13,500. The rest of the house was fairly flat in comparison except for a minor heave near the center of the opposite end of the home. The minor heave had slightly damaged the drywall. Our competitor misinterpreted the damage as showing settlement requiring underpinning and compaction grouting.

You don't have to be an elderly widow to become the victim of a deceptive or inadequate foundation investigation. A colleague told me about a case involving the owner of an apartment complex in my area that had obvious damage to a swimming pool. The owner hired a geotechnical engineer to document the conditions of the pool and the soil underneath it before hiring a contractor to perform compaction grouting. Seems like due diligence, right?

Unfortunately, the contractor did not engage a professional engineer to develop specifications and repair plans based on the documented conditions. That missed step is not unusual in foundation repair. It's where many contractors stumble. The pool shell turned out to be only four inches thick, which is extraordinarily thin. The soil below was composed of very wet clays and was very expansive. My colleague, who was working for the contractor at the time, had never done compaction grouting over wet expansive clays. He learned a lesson on the job: if you do not provide weep holes for the water to escape, you essentially are squeezing clays that already are very dense, and they are going to expand, pushing up on whatever is above. In this case, a fragile pool shell was in the way. It was so cracked and displaced that the owner ended up demolishing the pool.

Foundation repair can be a confusing enigma. You often get totally different approaches that arrive at very different solutions from different people. How do you figure out whose method is the best method? Thankfully, there is a consensus already in place in the industry. The Post-Tensioning Institute, the Foundation Performance Association (FPA), and the American Society of Civil Engineers (Texas Chapter) all have published standards. For

If you do not provide weep holes for the water to escape, you essentially are squeezing clays that already are very dense, and they are going to expand, pushing up on whatever is above.

example, the FPA defines three levels of investigation, ranging from a superficial walk-around to the rigorous testing and analysis that might be required for an insurance claim or as evidence in court. The middle level is not as rigorous but is still the thorough investigation homeowners need and deserve.

This chapter offers an overview of the many factors that come together to make up a thorough investigation. The next chapter will examine what the process is like when it is done right. Then in chapter

6, we will give you the inside scoop on how to avoid an investigation that is rushed, incomplete, or just plain fake or results in an expensive plan that's not a viable solution.

I have found that at least seventeen items must be accounted for in evaluating what's happening to a typical home with a potential foundation problem. Each element is bolded in the following three sections, which represent the three categories each element falls within—natural, structural, and procedural.

The Nature of the Problem

As we discussed in chapter 2, **soil** is the big natural factor underlying the settlement or heave that produces the symptoms that alert homeowners that they have a problem. So it's crucial to determine from as many sources as possible what the soil layer compositions and properties are under and around the house.

Precipitation is often soil's coconspirator in both heave and settlement. We all have a general idea how rainy, snowy, or arid our local climate is, but that's not specific enough. Diagnosing settlement or heave involves gathering long-term precipitation data and understanding its effect on soils at that particular location—as compared to other areas. The next chapter offers further explanation and examples beyond the truisms that rainwater and snowmelt don't run uphill.

We have discussed how soil gets pushed around and its layers transformed during construction, giving each house a unique *topography*. Our diagnosis requires understanding the original topography and modifications to the soil before and after the house was built.

The building's **age** is a factor in any diagnosis and understanding how long moisture migration under the foundation has been occurring.

Structural Issues

In chapter 2 we saw that different structural systems interact differently with various soil conditions. For our investigation, we must have a complete understanding of the structural systems and **load paths** of a home, including truss systems versus nontruss systems, interior load-bearing walls, and post-tensioned versus conventional versus pier-and-beam systems.

Of course, there can be substantial variations in the structural system from one house to another that we can understand only by having a complete **floor plan** drawn to scale.

Procedural Methods

Site photography, done systematically with a photo numbering plan that corresponds to floor plan numbering, is a hallmark of a thorough, organized investigation.

Aerial photography helps us understand drainage, landscaping, and all of the natural and structural changes that may have taken place around a house. It seems counterintuitive (if not silly) that you could learn about what's happening under a concrete slab by looking at available satellite maps and historical photos shot from an airplane or satellite. But the investigation requires seeing the big picture: How much sunshine and shade are around the house? What is the proportion of trees versus grass? Photos help us get expert analysis of structural damage related to the past conditions of the land unknown to, or forgotten by, the homeowner.

A complete *floor-level survey* with topographical mapping provides an understanding of topological patterns and their interpretations.

Our job would be easier if floors always deviated in only one direction from perfectly level (which they never start at from day one), but they don't just deflect that way. A complete **tilt and deflection analysis** interprets where and how much the foundation is above or below an acceptable level.

A complete **damage map** overlaid with the topographical map can help show how the damage relates to the observed elevations. Extensive experience is necessary to see the nuances in signs of damage because similar symptoms can have different causes, and the interpretation involves the effects of surrounding infrastructure.

At this point, we have a lot of data, and to make sense of it, we need a **compilation** to see how each item affects all of the others. The observations and recommendations supported by the data should be **written**. A **repair plan** adds specifications and placement of various recommended elements. Let's emphasize here that we just covered three separate steps that must be done methodically in this order for the plan to be evidence based and ready for review and execution.

Peer review is the best way to check all of the assumptions that went into the plan and to ensure that the conclusions in the report are supported by the data.

A licensed professional engineer can then approve the entire report by affixing a **seal**.

A Reality Check

Sometimes one of the many factors above seems to be the obvious culprit, or one part of the process seems to produce a smoking gun, justifying shortcuts in the investigation. That's a mistake. As we work through the entire process, many times we see findings that point to differing conclusions. Only by seeing how all of these findings work together can we start to construct a viable narrative about what has happened and make an appropriate repair plan.

The next chapter will take a deeper look at what's involved in doing a real investigation. "Deeper look" is more than a figure of speech here, as you might guess from all of our previous discussion of soil and groundwater. Actual digging may be involved.

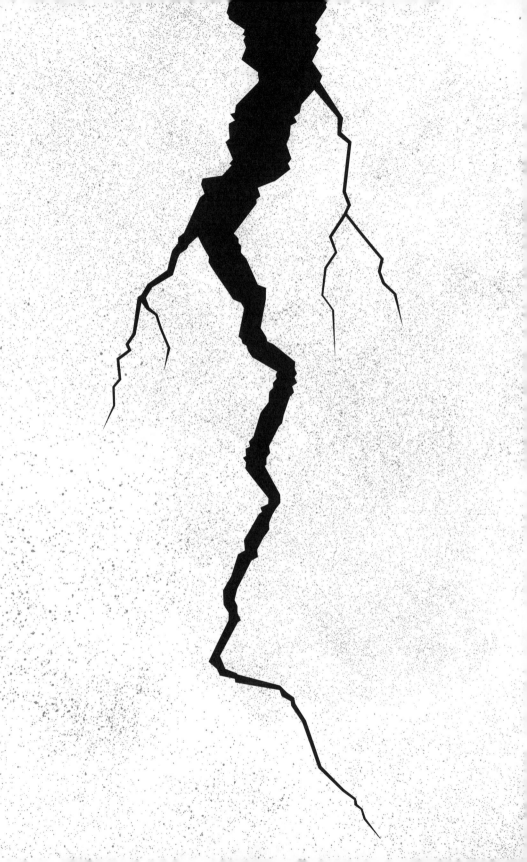

CHAPTER 5

UNCOVERING THE NITTY-GRITTY DETAILS

Note to the reader: This chapter has a lot of details about what is required to do a proper investigation. If you are not the detailed type, you don't really need to worry about understanding these, though this chapter may still be useful to you as a reference and if you want to dive even deeper, go to my website at www.foundationrepairsecrets.com. My main point with this chapter is to illustrate how complex and detailed an investigation needs to be in order to get it right—and how it is really impossible to do it on the spot while at the home.

I won't pretend that being a foundation repair contractor is glamorous, but it does involve a touch of Sherlock Holmes–style detective work. The investigator will look around the site and observe. Are there sidewalks on site that show signs of heaving? Are the soils exhibiting signs of expansive clays like shrinkage cracks?

I like to get a sample of soil from a few feet below the surface. Add water and roll it like a cigar; if it rolls up without falling apart, then it is clay. A cigar doesn't evoke the pipe-smoking detective, but in the first Holmes mystery novel, *A Study in Scarlet*, Watson says Sherlock can distinguish soils at a glance: "After walks, has shown me splashes upon his trousers and told me by their color and consistence in what part of London he had received them."

Study Site Soil Conditions

Given what we know about the behaviors of soils, any foundation investigation must start with an assessment of the known soil conditions. The more sources we can consider, the better our data will be. One of the primary sources of information is the soil survey published by the US Agriculture Department's Natural Resources Conservation Service. The survey is a fairly accurate map of known soil conditions for more than 95 percent of American counties. You can search and download different county maps at https://websoilsurvey.nrcs.usda.gov/app/. It usually gives information on a specific depth, the top five feet from the surface. Soil closer to the surface is called unburdened. If it is expansive clay, it can expand more when it is not burdened—buried under the weight and pressure of, say, twenty feet of soil.

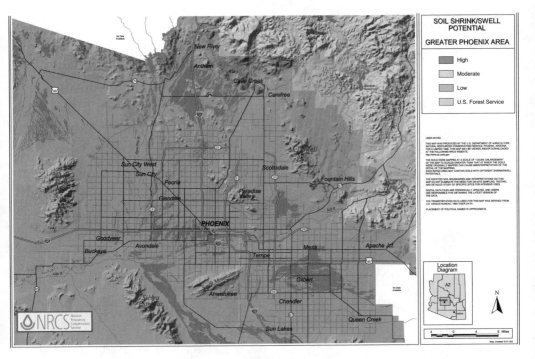

Figure 5.1: Soil map of the greater Phoenix area. Source: University of Arizona, Arizona Geological Survey, http://www.azgs.az.gov/files/phoenix-expansive-soils-nrcs144p2_064581.pdf.

Bear in mind that it would be a mistake to treat the official survey like a definitive final word. For example, I know of a particular area that has tremendous soil problems, but you wouldn't know if from the map because the original clays were deeper than five feet. Much of the upper soils were removed during development, leaving the unburdened, expansive clays near the surface, where they can easily heave.

The best soil information would be site specific, but that's usually not available. Sometimes reports from nearby sites can be useful. It helps to be familiar with the geography in the area. Historical aerial photography can help. Once you understand the soil layer compositions, you can use the information to understand whether the site has more potential for heave or settlement.

Determine Moisture and Temperature Patterns

Figure 5.2: National moisture map demonstrating average annual precipitation in inches. Source: www.GISGeography.com.

In order to understand what is happening with the soil, we must understand how historical moisture patterns have affected that soil. As explained in chapter 2, evapotranspiration is the process in which vapor rises from underground water sources. Water from rain and snow makes its way into the water table and into the soil in general. Over very long periods of time, the evapotranspirative cycle will make moisture levels in the soil somewhat constant, falling within general parameters, depending on the area's average rainfall. A grassroots volunteer network of backyard weather observers provides data and maps that you can find by searching for the Community Collaborative Rain, Hail & Snow Network.

An area with higher average precipitation is likely to have more moisture in its soil, but what does that mean for building foundations? As explained in chapter 2, the accumulation of moisture will affect the soil in different ways, including the one we called suction. To review: Clay soil has a negative ionic charge. Water has a positive one. As a result, they are attracted to each other. After heavy rain falls around a house sitting on a slab, moisture is attracted to much drier soil under the center.

Some general examples of the climate factor:

- Drier climates tend to accumulate moisture over time in the center of a slab on grade. In an area where the soil has long been relatively moist, additional precipitation would be less likely to cause that suction of moisture toward the center.

- During dry periods in wetter climates, loss of moisture around the perimeter could be an issue.

- In areas with snow accumulation, a more gradual moisture supply is introduced as the snow melts over time historically both before and after housing is erected.

- In desert climates with less plant life, the soil absorbs less with natural, undisturbed landscapes. With the introduction of suburban housing, the

Clay soil has a negative ionic charge. Water has a positive one. As a result, they are attracted to each other. After heavy rain falls around a house sitting on a slab, moisture is attracted to much drier soil under the center.

water is shed less efficiently and is absorbed more than in the past.

- Understand previous land use such as farming that might have residual moisture at depth.

Use Aerial Photography

As mentioned in the previous chapter, historical aerial photography can reveal valuable clues. These include past uses, prior water flows or rock formations, and topography changes. Historical aerial photos can sometimes show whether the site was once a riverbed or whether the site was filled. We came across evidence that one site we were looking at was filled with buried, bulldozed trees and then covered up with more fill! Studying photos taken in different years can reveal how soil conditions changed at a site, which helps us understand how various clays and other soils are moved and changed by human activity and perhaps discover forgotten geologic features at a site. There are a number of sources for historical aerial photos.

Trees pull moisture from soil under the foundation possibly inducing settlement

Irrigated grass is typically over watered possibly inducing heave

Pools many times have deco drains that trap water possibly inducing heave

Narrow side yards make poor drainage causing moisture to accumulate

Roofs draining to the sides exacerbate poor drainage and cause more moisture to accumulate

Figure 5.3

An overview of the current landscaping and layout of the site also is an important tool for diagnosing foundation problems. Among the reasons are the following:

- Trees steal moisture and sometimes have destructive uplifting roots.

- Irrigated grass usually adds water and usually is overwatered.

- Historical aerials show how long the pad sat in the sun before being built.

- Often house pads are overcompacted in order to pass inspection.

- Even when patios, driveways, pool decks, and the like have drainage systems installed, the drains often inject water into the soil.

- Narrow side yards accumulate water.

- Gabled roofs without gutters that dump into narrow side yards exacerbate poor drainage.

- AC units can discharge condensate lines near home perimeters.

Examine Site Topography

An investigation into the natural and altered topography of the site can yield good information to help shed light on what can be happening below the surface:

- Sloped topography can accumulate moisture on the high side.

- Fill areas can be candidates for settlement. Soil placed after being excavated, called *backfill*, will usually compress or consolidate over time, even if it has been somewhat compacted.

- Cut areas—where excavation has removed soil—can be candidates for heave.

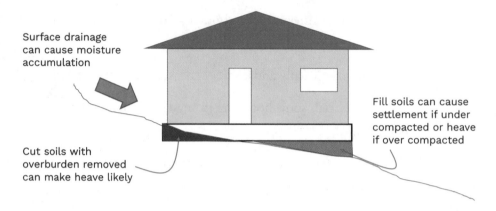

Surface drainage can cause moisture accumulation

Fill soils can cause settlement if under compacted or heave if over compacted

Cut soils with overburden removed can make heave likely

Figure 5.4: A house on a slope collects moisture from drainage on the high side.

I have seen, on rare occasions, cut areas that have been overexcavated accidentally during construction and filled back and undercompacted, leading to settlement. I have also seen fill areas filled with expansive soil and overcompacted, leading to heave. Those logic-defying cases are exceptions that prove the rule that you cannot rely on one or even a few isolated observations at a site. Code requires six inches of fall in the first ten feet. Most newer homes cannot meet this requirement, mostly because of space considerations, and are often compounded with smaller side yards and fencing.

Consider Foundation Types

The type of foundation plays a significant role in helping determine heave versus settlement. Let's look again at the three common types of foundations introduced in chapter 1:

- Floating floor slab

- Post-tensioned foundation

- Pier-and-beam foundation with a crawl space

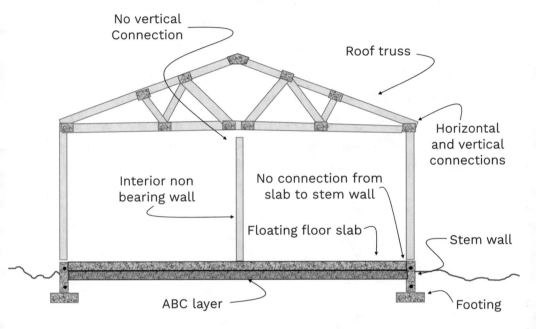

Figure 5.5: This drawing of a floating floor slab foundation shows that downward forces are heaviest on the footings.

The floor slab is a large area with very little weight on it. The footing, a relatively small area absorbing heavier downward pressure, can more easily push into the soil. If the footing settles and creates a void, the slab may follow, but usually only if a footing leads the way.

The same foundation design has an opposite scenario: the forces in the soil that push up have much more influence on a floor slab than they do on a footing. The area of the floor is large, with very little weight on it, leaving it susceptible to soil heaving. On the other hand, the footings have a smaller area, are lower, and are much less susceptible to heave.

Slabs heave more easily than footings, and footings settle more easily than slabs. Slabs may settle following footings but usually not on their own. Of course, there are always exceptions. On occasion, we have found a slab settling when a deep soil problem caused the soil to settle under its own weight, and the slab followed it.

Another exception involves the stem wall, a short wall that sits on top of the footing to support the frame or masonry wall above it. Poor backfilling within high stem walls (more than twenty-four inches) may result in floor slabs that settle without footing settlement, particularly where local practices use less-than-ideal fill such as cinder rock.

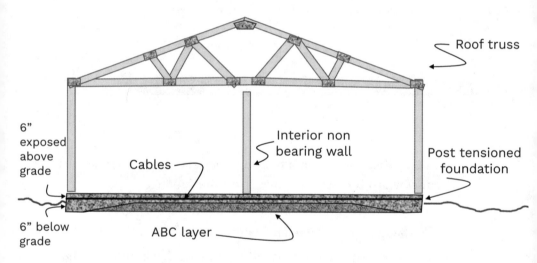

Figure 5.6: This drawing shows a type of post-tensioned foundation popular in the Southwest.

Post-tensioned (PT) foundations have gained in popularity over the past forty years. A particular type, the uniform thickness PT foundation, has gained prevalence in the Southwest. High strength cables run in both directions, spaced about thirty inches apart. These cables are tightened up to about thirty-three thousand pounds of force a few days after the concrete is poured. The tremendous force stretching the cables also squeezes the concrete, creating a slab that is very stiff but is still not immune to foundation problems.

Originally, PT systems had deep ribs with cables at both the top and the bottom. Since the cables hold the concrete in tension, this reinforcement kept the foundation system from deflecting or bending. The uniform thickness system is less robust in that it has one cable in the middle. (Engineers call this the neutral zone. Star Trek fans, this is not where the Romulans are.) The concrete above and below is not held by the cables and can crack in tension (and thus bend the slab) more easily. The other disadvantage of this particular system is that it has very little edge protection. Since it projects down very little (about six inches), water can penetrate around the edge and flow underneath very easily. As a result, soils are more easily affected by poor drainage. In addition, the PTI suggests designing for ideal conditions, which usually are not met in the long run.

With no isolated footings, the downward forces of the roof loads are spread across a larger area of the PT foundation, making it harder for settlement to happen. Because the slab is tied into the foundation monolithically, the entire system is much more at risk for heave, especially around the edges.

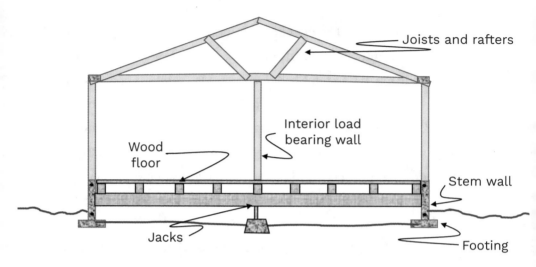

Figure 5.7: Pier-and-beam foundations are alternatives to slabs on grade.

As you might deduce from prior discussions, settlement is more likely than heave with pier-and-beam foundations because of the way the load is concentrated rather than distributed across a slab. These homes may have adjacent slabs, however, such as garages, patios, and sidewalks. These slabs are more vulnerable to heave and could move differently than connected portions of the home. I also have seen footings on the perimeter heave, despite being under the concentrated pressure of roof loads. If the footings are heaving, they must be on very expansive soil. Or the heave may be originating deep underground, resulting in it being spread over a larger area.

Older homes lack trusses to spread the roof loads only to the perimeter footings. The homes' interior walls pass the roof loads down to jacks under the crawl space. In this situation, interior floors can experience settlement more easily. But with the roof loads spread out more to many more points, the loads are not as concentrated, and heave is possible. Heave is more likely than settlement if there are trusses concentrating the loads to only the perimeter and the interior jacks under the floor have only floor loads on them.

Follow the weight! Where there are concentrated loads, settlement is more likely than heave— the more load, the more likely. Conversely, with lighter loads, heave is more likely. When slabs and footings are not mechanically connected, there could be opportunities for them to move separately or even in opposite directions.

Follow the weight! Where there are concentrated loads, settlement is more likely than heave—the more load, the more likely.

Use Floor Plans Drawn to Scale

Figure 5.8

Having floor plans drawn accurately and to scale is a lot more important than you might think. Many foundation assessments have plans that read "NTS," meaning "not to scale." But knowing exactly where kitchen cabinetry and bathroom fixtures are shows where the plumbing lines run in relation to the site's topography. The plumbing trenches may not be compacted thoroughly and can act as conduits for moisture to move through and are possible locations for leaks. Using a floor plan that is not to scale with topo-mapping software (discussed in the next section) can lead to incorrect conclusions. It's also important to know where utilities enter the house and the locations of closets, windows, doors, air conditioners, pool equipment, outside sidewalks, and patios. All can play roles in developing repair plans.

Also, it is important to know whether there are trusses versus joists and rafters, and in which directions they run, as well as the location of any interior-bearing walls. As explained in the previous section, if interior-bearing walls holding up the roof loads affect heaviness, they make settlement or heave more or less likely under those walls, respectively.

Look at Floor Topo Map Patterns

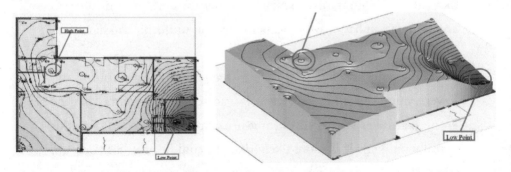

Figures 5.9 and 5.10: Foundation topo mapping

We already have discussed studying the topography of the site where a home was built, but we also use topography mapping of interior floors. Topography is the graphical representation of the elevation differences using curving lines on a map. A topographical map displaying the patterns—combined with an accurate floor plan and floor elevation readings that take into account different floor coverings—is a main tool in diagnosing foundation problems. The topo map can look like a bunch of amoebas floating around. But seeing a series of topo lines in proximity, like zebra stripes, indicates significant consistent elevation change worth paying attention to. The highs and lows depicted on the map don't automatically show what has moved up or down, because they are only relative readings, not absolute elevations. In other words, the numbers have meaning only in how they relate to each other. But the patterns on the map can help explain the movement of the foundation or floor slab.

Let's envision this typical situation: a relatively flat slab has one low area on the perimeter, which is bearing the roof loads, and that area shows damage associated with settlement. If most of the slab is relatively flat, with one area that is lower, it is reasonable to assume that the lower area has dropped. This observation should be supported with additional data in order to be conclusive, but it is a lot more likely than the alternative explanation that the entire rest of the slab and foundation has heaved in a perfectly flat, uniform, and harmonious way.

Now contrast this to a pattern that shows fairly uniform and lower around the entire perimeter. Is it reasonable to assume that the entire perimeter settled uniformly in perfect harmony? Again, this is really unlikely. It is more likely that the middle area has risen up. That's a classic heave pattern, but there are exceptions to every rule.

Suppose the topo survey shows low on one side and high on the other. Has the high side moved up, or has the low side moved down? Without more data, there is no clear interpretation.

> You can see how, with all the work that is required, it is impossible for a nonengineer to do all this in one visit. And we still have more to cover!

Interpret Signs of Stress

Figure 5.11

Most pour-out strips don't protrude like this, but this photograph illustrates the stress from slab movement. Since the door frame sits on top of the pour-out strip and is part of the floor slab, an outside door that is out of square or pinched could equally be a result of either footing movement or slab movement.

Homeowners typically call in a foundation contractor or engineer after noticing signs of stress, such as cracking walls. We view the signs of stress not so much as problems in and of themselves but rather as clues to the types of movement and their meaning. Generally, where we have measured and mapped a high spot in the floor (meaning the high areas of the slab, as shown by the topo mapping), damage indicates upward movement in that area of the structure, whereas conversely damage correlating to lower spots indicates downward movement. If a floor is sloping, the lowest point may not be where the problem is. The problem may be where the downward angle starts, the hinge point. Damage to either the interior or exterior of heavily loaded perimeter walls is a likely sign of settlement. Damage to interior walls that do not have footings or bear any roof loads usually indicates heave because those walls are up higher than footings, have a large contact area with the soil, and are lightly loaded. The same logic applies to interior doors out of square (pinched on one side or showing a gap on the other).

Exterior doors are a separate case because of what we call pour-out strips. That's where a notch in the stem wall allows the slab to extend out under the threshold of an exterior door. In that case, vertical joints between the stem wall and interior floor slab do not run directly under the door threshold. Signs of stress at the door cannot be assumed to be settlement and could result from slab movement caused by heave.

Windows out of square almost always indicate footing movement because they rarely sit on top of the interior slab. It's worth noting that walls might have been patched in the past and doors shaved off to alleviate a pinch, but because windows usually are not replaced for being out of square, they are a more consistently visible sign of footing movement.

> - Interior signs of stress in walls, doors, and windows usually signal interior floor heave.
> - Exterior signs of stress in walls, doors, and windows usually indicate footing settlement.
> - An important exception is exterior door frame movement, which can equally signal footing settlement or floor slab heave.
> - Windows are better indicators than other signs of stress, such as cracks in walls or doors out of square.

There are a few more signs of stress not involving walls, doors, and windows.

Sometimes drywall becomes uneven at its intersection with the ceiling in a pattern called cupping. It usually happens when the interior wall is pushed up into the ceiling. Where the drywall meets only drywall in the ceiling, it pushes up more easily than in spots where it encounters resistance—where the bottoms of the trusses are located.

Figure 5.12: Cupping occurs in an interior drywall that is being pushed up into a ceiling where the bottoms of the trusses resist it.

More rarely, downward movement of a perimeter wall could result in cupping. More regularly, we see cracks in the corners where interior walls meet the perimeter walls. What is happening typically is that the roof-load-bearing exterior walls are holding steady, while the interior walls are moving upward because they are subject to heave in the center of the home, and they start to pull away at the bottom. Alternatively, and more rarely, if the outside wall footing settles, it can pull away from interior walls.

Other clues to watch for are gaps under the baseboards or the floor pushing them up from below, which we call cramming of baseboards.

> • The cupping of trusses usually indicates the heaving of interior walls, hence the heaving of the floor slabs.

> - Corner cracks between interior and perimeter walls usually indicate the heaving of interior walls and floors.
> - The cramming of baseboards usually indicates floor heaving.

Relate Photos to Floor Plan

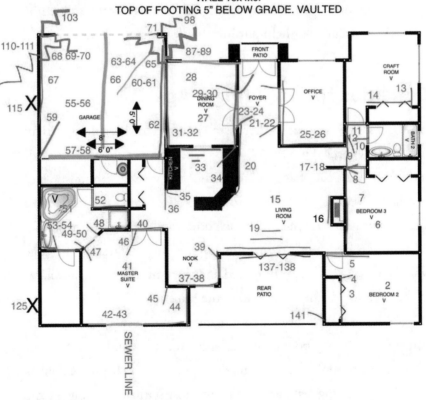

Figure 5.13: This floor plan has color-coded damage markings and photo numbers for easy reference.

It is handy to mark up the floor plan so the photos and the damage that they record are easy to associate with their respective locations. In the example shown, blue lines indicate ceiling cracks, red lines indicate wall cracks, and green lines indicate floor cracks. The "greater than" sign points in the direction of pinched doors or windows. For example, suppose a door is out of square and has a gap below its hinge side while dragging on the floor toward the side with the handle or knob. That's the pinched direction in which the ">" would be pointing. Pinched interior doors are likely indicators of heave, so the symbols are important to the investigation. Uniform symbols and *nomenclature* and eye-catching photos make it easier to put together a mental picture of what is happening. The human brain is aided by heuristic shortcuts that help put information together like a puzzle.

Consider the Building's Age

How old is the structure? There is a lot more to this question than you might expect. First the obvious: Older homes show more wear and tear because they have had more time to interact with soils, wind, thermal movement, and other forces of deterioration. Over time, these forces accumulate, interact with each other, and weaken the structure.

My experience in Arizona, however, is that it starts on the edge where moisture is first encountered and then, over time, accumulates to the middle. The heaving follows the moisture.

With soil that has been dry for many years, that edge heave starts in homes with typically poor drainage, added watering, and all of the four mechanisms of moisture accumulation described in chapter 2. Unless there is a plumbing leak, accumulation must start on the edge of the foundation. Almost all of the newer foundations that we have measured over the years have edge heave where the edge goes up from swelling soils.

The question I wanted to answer was whether the edge heave occurred because the homes were new or because of the designs of most of the new homes were using the post-tensioned (PT) slabs. Personally, I have seen very few PT foundation systems with center heave. They were all homes approaching twenty years old or older. But I regularly see examples of newer, conventional-foundation types with edge heave. My evidence is more anecdotal than conclusive so far but does point away from design as the cause of the early onset edge heave.

I have performed multiple floor-level surveys over more than ten years on the same conventional-foundation house, using a subtractive topo to delineate the movement over time. Clearly what started out as an edge heave within the first ten to fifteen years shifted toward a center heave.

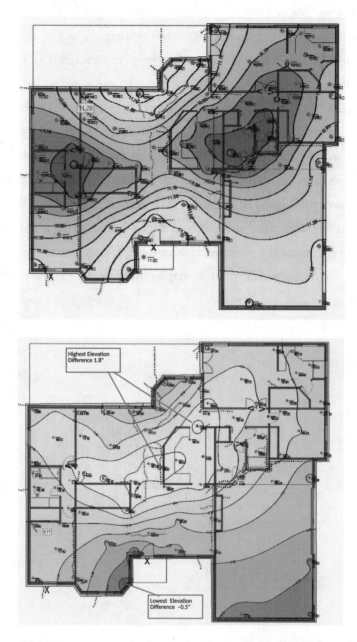

Figure 5.14: Topo maps of a house with a conventional foundation show how moisture accumulation moved over the years from the edges (lighter shading on top map) toward the center.

How Bad Is Bad?

The purpose of all this careful, detailed analysis is not to produce a report full of numbers and charts but to reach sound conclusions. So the house is two inches lower in one area versus another. Does that mean it needs underpinning? Not necessarily. I have seen houses up to nine inches out of level with very little damage and houses an inch or two out of level with much more damage. What gives? The nine-inch elevation difference was just a steady, even tilt of a house with a very rigid slab. The house with extensive damage had a huge bulge in the profile of the footing and floor.

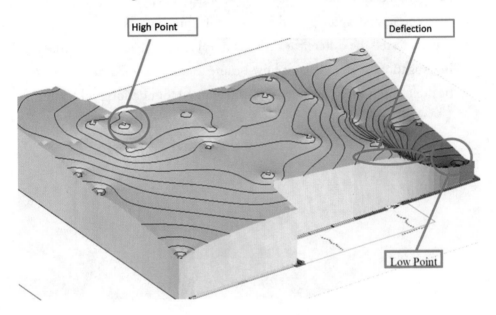

Figure 5.15

That bulge is called *deflection*. When engineers measured the deflection and drew the results on a graph that showed deviation from a straight line, there was no such stress indictor for the home with very little damage—just a nice, even slope. Structures can withstand a lot of tilt as compared with deflection.

How much tilt or deflection is too much? The Foundation Performance Association and the Post-Tensioning Institute have guidelines that I believe should be followed unless a new and better consensus is more widely accepted. But following the guidelines requires plotting the data points, filling in the contours, and accurately determining deflection or tilt. Many forensic experts have issues with this particular definition of deflection. They perhaps correctly claim that it does not follow the classic definition of any deviation from a straight line. Because of this, certain conditions can be exaggerated, such as a deviation near the edge. Perhaps over time a better guideline can be more widely accepted.

The next chapter provides a way for homeowners who are not experts to tell the difference between a real and a pseudoengineering investigation. It also explains how I came to realize something had to be done about the prevalence of misdiagnosed foundation problems.

CHAPTER 6

DON'T GET HOODWINKED
BY A FAKE INVESTIGATION

Dean Kruger was running a nice business pouring concrete when he decided he could expand by addressing a big problem in his market. He would start repairing stem walls. And just like that, Kruger became a foundation repair contractor—never mind the fact that stem walls are aboveground and that he had never driven a pile into the ground. In other words, he was less of an expert on foundation-related soil movement than any reader of this book who has gotten this far along.

Kruger was not a modest or cautious fellow, so he didn't hesitate to tell homeowners when he thought they had settlement problems. He didn't know anything about soil mechanics or structural engineering, but he was a good salesman. He could say with confidence that he had been working on foundations for many years. He just didn't mention the part about only pouring or patching concrete.

Kruger knew that people trust photographic evidence, and he knew how to use a camera and produce videos that showed fear-inducing damage. In his presentations, in person or online, he was the *only* guy who knew how to properly fix your foundation problem, using what happened to be the limited methods he knew. Kruger also had a strong competitive instinct, so he didn't hesitate to knock down advice a homeowner may have gotten from another contractor. At this point I should make clear that I am not talking about a real person, but a bogeyman I made up, but he is a composite of several individuals like him out there. I named him after the Dunning-Kruger effect, a term that psychologists use for the tendency of the least educated or skilled people to have the most confidence in their knowledge or abilities.

How can homeowners protect themselves from becoming victims in a Kruger horror film? The short answer is to make sure contractors are following industry standards, not some standards they made up for themselves. Homeowners should not be expected to be foundation experts. They should ask some basic questions and demand answers in plain language that they can understand. This chapter provides a relatively short guide for evaluating whether a contractor is going to follow an industry-standard protocol designed to protect homeowners.

The short answer is to make sure contractors are following industry standards, not some standards they made up for themselves.

Questions Homeowners Can Ask

1. Do you get paid based on how much work you find is needed?

   Most foundation repair salespeople are compensated directly or indirectly on the dollar value of the repairs they recommend. They may be earning commissions or have their job performance evaluated based on recommended repairs, which is at least a potential conflict of interest. This also applies to owners of a foundation repair company who also get paid for each sale.

2. What formal training have you received in how to do this inspection?

   Most foundation repair salespeople receive training only from their suppliers. Few have earned university degrees in soil mechanics or structural engineering. Years of experience doing the same thing don't cut the mustard comparatively.

3. Is the analysis done on the spot?

   I have met hundreds of licensed, professional engineers over the years and made a point of always asking them this question: "Would you be comfortable in going to a home and coming up with a repair plan on the spot?" Not one of them said yes because further research and consultation is always needed.

4. Are the recommendations coming from a licensed design professional?

   When a problem is identified and solutions presented, the Post-Tensioning Institute says the evaluations, recommendations, and repair plans should come from a licensed design professional. This is not the same as having an engineer sign off on calculations for pile spacing on a permit application after the repair plan has been arrived at—see the end of chapter 2.

5. What industry recognized inspection protocols are you following?

Are you following the Post-Tensioning Institute standard? Or the Foundation Performance Association's? Or any recognized standard? Many foundation repair salespeople don't even know about these.

6. How will you gauge the problem's severity?

If industry-accepted consensus standards are not being used to judge the severity of the problem, then the recommended plan of action carries no credible weight. It is merely an opinion, often formed by a salesperson with an incentive to sell products and services.

7. Does your company offer multiple solutions for both settlement and heave?

If a company's products and services can remediate settlement but not heave, the salesperson has a bias toward interpreting the evidence in that direction. The inspection findings may be factually accurate, but since no one wants to go home hungry, the resulting recommendations may be aimed at the wrong target.

8. Does your company have reviews or ratings vouching for the quality of its investigations?

Homeowners often go online to check out a company's reputation. Having testimonials or five-star ratings for performing repairs does not address whether the company is properly doing the investigation, analysis, and recommendations that should come first.

9. How objective is this investigation?

This question provides another, less confrontational way of asking again for assurance that the investigation is not poorly informed or biased. If the contractor cannot explain in detail how the inspection will result in data-driven conclusions, then the homeowner is just getting a nebulous opinion.

10. How can I be assured that the initial recommendations are followed?

Will the engineer who made the recommendations for the problems discovered sign and seal a letter approving of the final product to solve the problem he or she diagnosed?

An Insider's View

A contractor proposing ideas and processes that differ from some industry norms, as I am doing in this book, also has questions to answer. Where did those ideas come from? How did those processes develop, and what makes them work? Let me take a step back and start answering those questions.

About twenty-four years ago, one of the large providers of foundation repair services approached my company, Arizona Repair Masons, to join a national network of dealers of its product. I had been doing *mud jacking*, which is pumping a mudlike mixture under the concrete to level a slab. I didn't know much about underpinning or how to evaluate structures for soil-caused movement. So I took my cue from my supplier and used the Oklahoma-based company's system to install piers where there were low areas and cracks. There was not much discussion of heave.

In 2013 I quit that supplier dealer and signed on with Foundation Supportworks, a national home-repair-product supplier based in Nebraska. The training from Supportworks was great but still involved very little discussion of expansive soil heave except to explain bowing basement walls.

The foundation industry has been around for more than fifty years. Most of its equipment manufacturers sprang up in areas that have relatively wet climates with variable but substantial precipitation. Those companies helped develop and spread underpinning techniques that proved over the years to be largely very effective. There are many manufacturers and suppliers and their associated installers, and some systems are a little better than others.

Figure 6.1: Holes dug to access the below-grade footings to install piles

Figure 6.2: Holes being dug to install pile brackets on footings

Figure 6.3: Bracket installed under footing with pile in the bracket

Figure 6.4: Piles being driven to refusal using a hydraulic driving cylinder

Figure 6.5 After piles are driven to refusal, hydraulics are used to lift and level using hydraulic lifting cylinders together in series.

Chapter 4 briefly explained underpinning, but let's take a closer look to see why I found it was often not the answer to foundation problems in the desert climate where I live and work. Underpinning is the process of driving piles, typically helical or push piles, down through the various soil layers until it reaches a load-bearing *stratum*, which basically is really hard soil or rock. Engineers call this driving the piles "to *refusal.*"

Instead of the footing loads bearing on unreliable soils, where water can penetrate, those soils are bypassed and the loads transferred to the piles via a mechanical bracket. This is shown pictorially in figure 6.5. Once the house is stabilized on its new supports, it can be releveled (more or less—see below) and supplemented with either grout injection or *polyurethane* foam injection under the slabs.

The underpinning work typically starts with digging a hole about three feet deep outside of the home to access the existing footing.

The footing gets notched so that an L-shaped bracket can fit under it directly under the wall. The bracket protects the edge of the existing footing from stress.

Once all of the piles are driven, hydraulic systems can be used to raise and relevel the home. I say, "more or less," because many homes were never level to start with or, for various reasons, cannot be made perfectly level. But if settlement had caused the foundation problem, usually it stops, gaps can be filled, and cracks can be closed up. Unfortunately, that happy ending did not always match the reality I was experiencing.

As I have established in previous chapters, misdiagnoses of foundation problems are significant occurrences. Many homes have floor heave, and I wanted to know the best way to deal with it. That quest turned into a lengthy research and development project for my company. We found no model to emulate, no training available, no rules to follow, and no consensus standards. We developed our own objective standards over six years' time, along with proprietary software to streamline the process and provide quality control.

The process was rigorous but risky from a business perspective. Every foundation repair contractor we talked with about what we were doing, as well as our own supplier, told us the model was unsustainable and would never be profitable. We hung in there in the belief that if we did right by the customers, we would be rewarded.

Now what happens if the homeowner contracts for a real investigation, and the careful analysis concludes there is a floor slab heave and no footing movement? In the next chapter, I will lay out the options, including the revolutionary process developed by our team.

CHAPTER 7

HOW TO REMEDIATE A HEAVE

The quarter-inch crack where one of the interior and exterior walls met in a big suburban ranch house was a problem that I thought I could repair easily enough. I arrived with three workers to help dig up the gravel-covered side yard to access the foundation footing about two feet underground. We would attach an *L*-shaped bracket to the footing every eight feet on that side of the house. The brackets would each hold a steel pile that was two and seven-eighths inches in diameter. We would use hydraulic cylinders to gently push the piles into the ground until they reached really hard soil or rock.

This underpinning job happened early in my career, so we dug with shovels, not an excavating machine. I probably had a walkie-talkie or flip phone to talk to the crew as I stood with the homeowner inside as the workers used the piles to start to lift the house just about an inch. At that point in the process, it should have taken less than five minutes to reverse the sinking of the footing and close that big wall crack in the corner of the room where we were standing.

"Hey, stop! It's getting worse!" the homeowner yelled. He was right. I stayed calm because I knew we could just lower the house back down, which we did. That's when I suppose I said what any foundation repair contractor would say in that situation: "It's not a problem. The home just needed stabilization, not lifting, and the underpinning will do the job." This was many years before I really understood about expansive soils and remediating heave. We followed what our supplier told us to do in installing the piles. Realizing now what happened, we tried to lift the edge of a house that had heave in the center, adding stress rather than relieving it. The crack got worse because it was not caused by settlement of the footing lowering the exterior wall. It was caused by heave pushing up the interior wall.

Some years later, when I first started thinking about all of the misdiagnoses of soil-related damage, I knew floor slab heave was clearly responsible for the majority of it in the arid climates I was most familiar with. But most foundation repair contractors didn't want to talk about heave remediation. There was a simple reason. They didn't have really viable solutions.

They generally could offer five options:

- Install cutoff walls.

- Perform leak repairs.

- Remove and replace the interior slab.

- Provide grading and drainage improvements.

- Perform excavation lowering.

We'll walk through those so that you can compare them with the approach we developed over the years involving soil venting.

Installing Cutoff Walls

Placing walls into the ground around a house creates a barrier to stop water from going under the perimeter. Installation involves excavating a five-foot-wide-by-one-foot-deep trench all around the house. Within the wide trench, a narrower trench is dug four feet deep to provide a moisture barrier. Plastic is then run from the bottom of the trench to the house, where it is attached to the edge of the stem wall.

The process is intrusive, in that air-conditioning units, pool pumps, sidewalks, plants, irrigation, and all underground utilities must be moved. We have installed many cutoff walls, with the cost to homeowners generally running from $55,000 to $150,000. Cutoff walls can successfully stop the encroachment of moisture—or reduce it since the sealing is not 100 percent effective, and water can still penetrate or go underneath them. The downside, besides the cost and disruption, is that excessive moisture also cannot get out from under the house. If there is a leak, for example, heave could get worse.

Figure 7.1: Digging a trench around a house like this to install a cutoff wall is expensive and time consuming. This picture also shows excavation lowering, explained later.

Removing and Replacing Interior Slab

Figure 7.2: Removal and replacement of the interior slab is even more expensive and more intrusive.

Replacing the slab basically requires gutting the entire interior of the house, including the floors, all cabinetry, and plumbing fixtures before rebuilding it. The cost can run from $100,000 to $300,000. Of course, the residents of the home also must move out for the duration of the process. Not fun. Once the slab is out, it's possible to dig out and replace the expansive soils underneath to remediate the heave. But this solution is usually not cost effective.

Providing Grading and Drainage Improvements

Maintaining proper drainage and limiting the moisture intrusion under a slab on houses built in the arid Southwest is a good practice we often recommend. These improvements can help with a heave problem but fail to fix it because the effect is not large enough on the specific area experiencing the problem, which is the interior center area. Depending on the scope, this work can range from relatively cheap to somewhat expensive. Just adding or replacing gutters can run $10,000 to $20,000 at this time in my area.

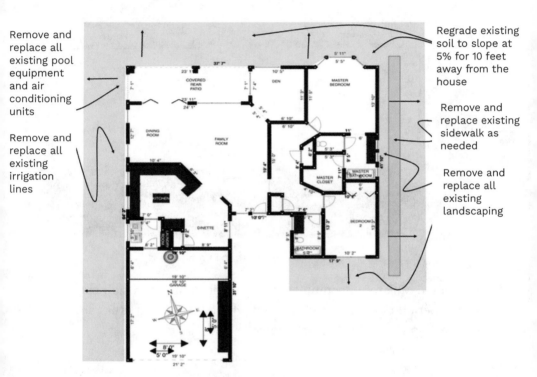

Remove and replace all existing pool equipment and air conditioning units

Remove and replace all existing irrigation lines

Regrade existing soil to slope at 5% for 10 feet away from the house

Remove and replace existing sidewalk as needed

Remove and replace all existing landscaping

Figure 7.3: This drawing shows an extensive plan for improving grading and drainage.

If the soil under the slab is wetter in the middle and drier on the edges, drying the edges could actually be counterproductive. Moisture accumulates over long periods of time. If it has built up under the middle of the slab, that is the area of the heave. Installing gutters and improving drainage around the perimeter of a home can dry and shrink clay soil on the perimeter, increasing the differential in moisture and elevation between the edge and the center of the slab. Rather than flattening the slab, it worsens the heave problem at least temporarily before eventually being helpful.

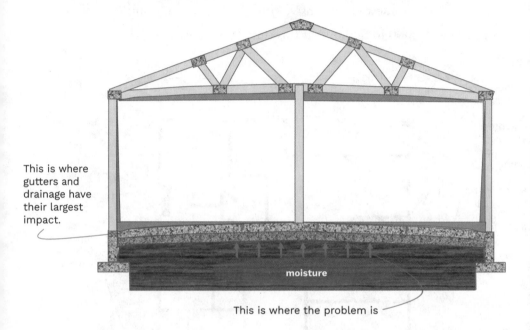

This is where gutters and drainage have their largest impact.

moisture

This is where the problem is

Figure 7.4: Moisture accumulates under the center of a slab over a long period of time, but that is not where installing gutters and drainage improvements dries the soil.

Performing Excavation Lowering

Clearing out the soil under a house after underpinning it with piles is called excavation lowering. We have done many excavation-lowering projects over the past sixteen years. I pioneered this concept and still believe it is effective. But it is also expensive and intrusive, costing homeowners in my area $40,000 to $150,000. The photo that showed a trench for a cutoff wall also shows how the soil under the house was excavated at least twenty feet across (and in some places, all the way across) the foundation. That left the house sitting aboveground, supported only by the piers. Conventional slabs can be underexcavated in a limited way, but for the most part, they don't lend themselves to this kind of operation, so it really works mostly on post-tensioned slabs.

Finding a Better Way

Over the years, I not only used the four methods above but also worked on many new ideas—without much success. Now I am pleased to say that I have developed a solution that is cost effective, efficient, and nonintrusive. It is a revolutionary concept that I have pioneered with geotechnical engineer David Deatherage and the Arizona State University Geotechnical Department.

I had a discussion with Dave about work he did years earlier to remediate chemical pollution. From 1989 to 1995, Dave was working in the environmental industry on the problem of leaks from underground storage tanks. His technique was called soil venting, which was basically removing chemicals in the soil. When he did it underneath a building, the chemical removal was successful, but it had a side effect. As you have learned earlier in the book, drying out clay soils can cause them to shrink, which caused the building to settle. We then put our heads together and thought, "Why can't we use this same concept to control the soils?" That was the origin of the idea of using soil venting to

Drying out clay soils can cause them to shrink, which caused the building to settle. We then put our heads together and thought, "Why can't we use this same concept to control the soils?"

control heave, but developing a process took a lot of work during ensuing years.

MoistureLevel® Smart Foundation System

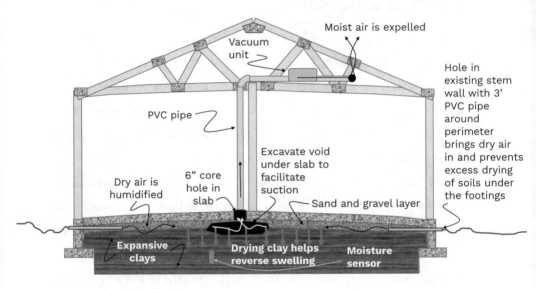

Figure 7.5: This concept drawing shows how the MoistureLevel® Smart Foundation System works.

This is a patented technology that we are making available to anyone with floor slab heave. The idea is to force dry air across the soil. Moisture collected in the aggregate base level or gravel layer under the concrete slab humidifies the dry air. The moisture is then vented out the stack.

As the soil becomes drier, it begins to suck the moisture out of the adjacent clays. As the clays begin to dry out, they develop cracks, which then dries out the soil near the crack, causing it to get wider and deepen and continue to make more cracks, generating a self-reinforcing cycle. Over time, the clays begin to lose their moisture and cease to expand, and often the soil contracts, reversing the swelling that caused the slab to heave.

The system has protections to minimize any overdrying near the footing area. It also has a smart mechanism that monitors the soil moisture content and regulates the drying to prevent overdrying.

The system is easy to install, usually taking less than a day, and typically costs less than one-twentieth the cost of other, less effective measures of heave control. Some more benefits include the following:

- It controls moisture of the clays under the slab on an ongoing basis, providing better long-term confidence than other repair-type solutions.

- It controls the indoor air quality for radon, a radioactive gas, and other potentially harmful gases and pollutants that could enter a house from the ground.

- It controls the problems of wet slabs, including delaminating tile, mold, and slab curling.

- There is some evidence, although unconfirmed at this point, that removing moisture under the slab provides some control for termites.

What It Looks Like

This installation process typically takes two workers less than a day. The occupants don't have to move out or even leave the home during the work. No furniture typically has to be moved because, as you are about to see, the work can take place in three out-of-the-way areas.

Figure 7.6: Intake ports are drilled into the outside stem wall.

The process starts simply enough, with drilling a one-inch diameter hole horizontally in the stem wall, and then proceeding to drill into the gravel layer that's underneath the slab. We perforate a PVC pipe with holes all around it and poke it through the stem wall. An upside-down P-trap on the outside of the pipe prevents it from taking in water from outside if there is a flood. The pipes are placed to serve as intake ports, bringing outside air in to dry the soil where moisture is causing expansive clays to heave. It's not rocket science, but the placement of each part of the system must be customized for each house after a careful study of both the structure and the soil conditions. We know from the floor-level survey where the high spots are that were created by the expansive soil heave. We dig a suction pit under the slab as close as possible to the highest spot of the heave to collect the moisture to be vented upward.

Figure 7.7: A closet near the high point of the slab is a typical place to drill a six-inch core hole in the slab to vent the soil.

We usually can place a four-inch vertical PVC pipe inconspicuously in a utility closet, pantry, or clothes closet to carry the moist air upward from the suction pit through a core hole we create in the slab. If that's impossible, a more expensive alternative is to go outside under the footing and bore in and do the venting on the exterior of the home.

Figure 7.8: The roof or attic can house the vacuum unit to suck out the moisture.

A small vacuum unit runs continuously to pull moisture through the PVC riser to be vented outdoors. It's a plastic box installed high above the suction pit in an attic or rooftop. The vacuum fan is low noise and uses no more electricity than a light bulb. We have been using a low-voltage model to save the cost of having an electrician wire it. Similar technology has long been used for radon gas removal.

For years, foundation contractors tried to remediate soil heave with costly, intrusive excavation and wall building. Occasionally they even gutted homes to dig out the heave, or more often they sold home-owners on grading and drainage improvements around the home that threatened to worsen the heave by drying out and sinking the perimeter. Finally, we have a revolutionary solution for remediating a heave cost effectively. The next chapter explains how we scientifically verified the success of the process during and since its development.

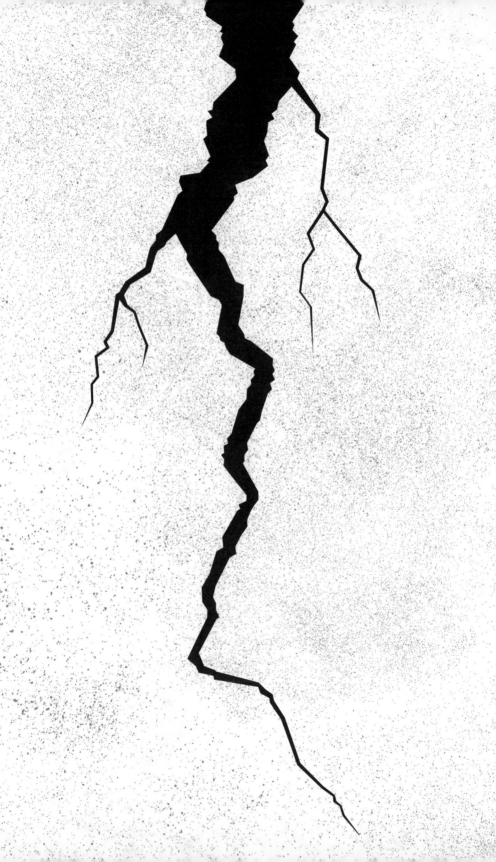

CHAPTER 8

VERIFICATION OF MOISTURELEVEL® WITH DATA

Since 2014 we have commercially installed about two thousand MoistureLevel® systems, as of this writing. That number does not include our experimental work dating back to 2004. What the number does reflect is the astounding number of homeowners in my greater Phoenix and Tucson areas who were clearly looking for a solution for expansive soil heave. Because each home is different, and because we have to customize foundation repair to specific circumstances, we take many measurements. Over time, the resulting data can be used to scientifically verify our success. Deatherage, the geotechnical engineer who helped develop the system, wrote a white paper[2] analyzing the data from a random sampling of twenty-nine installations from 2016 and sixty-two from 2019.

---

2   J. David Deatherage and Bob Brown, "Development and Engineering Aspects of the AZFS MoistureLevel Smart Foundation System" (white paper), November 12, 2019, https://cdn2.hubspot.net/hubfs/4187392/MoistureLevel%20Smart%20Foundation%20System%20White%20Paper.pdf.

Two things we could easily measure were the relative flatness of the slab and the amount of water being removed from the suction pit under the slab. The flatness is measured with floor-level manometer surveys corrected for different flooring thickness over slabs and is accurate to plus or minus one-tenth of an inch. Comparing repeated manometer surveys over time is extremely valuable in monitoring ongoing slab movements. We also measured the system suction in inches of water, average velocity of the exhaust pipe, exhaust air temperature and relative humidity, ambient air temperature and relative humidity, and ambient air intake ports' suction.

Results over Time

After crunching the numbers, the 2016 installations showed an average daily removal of water from under the floor slab of 17.3 pounds per day, which is a little over two gallons. The 2019 installs showed an average daily water removal of 68.8 pounds, which is more than eight gallons. (See the white paper referenced in footnote 2 to see the actual data.) Why the difference? Deatherage revised his research method to see both short-term and longer-term effects. The 2016 readings were made on existing systems after eight to twenty-six months of operation, while the 2019 readings were made at the initial installation of the systems. Other reasons for the higher removal rates include improvement of several important aspects of the systems: the size and number of the suction pits, increased the vacuum system suction and speed, improved intake piping configurations, and our learning to seal up better.

Sealing any cracks in the slab or gaps where air can come in easily close to the suction pit has proven crucial to the performance of the MoistureAir® system. Suction naturally will pull from the easiest spot, so an air leak creates a short circuit in the suction and detracts from it pulling moisture from the soil.

It is inconvenient to homeowners and expensive for us to keep returning to a home to measure the relative floor-level flatness, but we did monitor that data in many homes. Computer software plots the floor elevation points we have measured into a chart with topographic lines and colors indicating where it's high and where it's low. Comparing the numerical values at different points in time shows the average change, and the charting tells us visually what has happened with foundation movement. Since no slab is poured perfectly flat to start with and the original variations go unrecorded, having elevation measurements and observations of structural damage over time tells us more than we could learn from our initial floor-level survey.

We were able to look at long-term changes (forty-four to sixty months) for four sites, and their average flatness improved by one-fourth of an inch after excluding effects of other improvements, such as underpinning. The average for all sixty of the monitored sites included many performances that did not change at all, which we count as a victory because the main reason for installing the system is to stop future heaving. But in many instances, we saw a half-inch increase in flatness, and a few had more than an inch of increase in flatness. In eight of the monitored sites, the flatness got worse, probably due to short circuiting, embedded clays too deep for our system to reach (more than eight feet deep), or other installation issues that were less than optimal.

The monitoring helped us improve the system. Seeing patterns of movement over several years showed us that in a couple of cases we were starting to get the slab even flatter than it started out, requiring patching of gaps. To save homeowners from that trouble and expense, we introduced a two-speed vacuum that automatically kicks down to a lower maintenance speed when the soil dries out to a lower moisture percentage.

A Simple Visualization

To help you understand the patterns we are studying, I will show you a typical result we see over time with the installation of the MoistureLevel System. This is a good example to examine because the home had a distinct dome-heave pattern, and no work was done to remediate it other than installation of the MoistureLevel System. Computer software has mapped the topography of floor elevation readings, and I have highlighted the high and low elevation points.

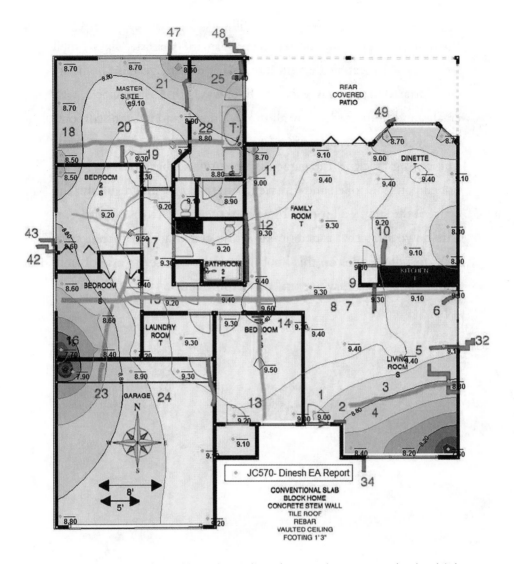

Figure 8.1: On this original reading (November 3, 2016), the high areas are the dining room, kitchen, and master bedroom—the middle-back area of the home.

The dome heave was fairly simple to diagnose. The house was thirty-five years old and located in an area with expansive clays. Small red lines on the graphic that indicate distress or damage in the home are concentrated in the areas where the floor was high. Ceiling cracks, wall cracks, and floor cracks were all in the kitchen and master bedroom. The few exterior cracks were minor and in the high-elevation areas. The ceiling crack in the garage is not unusual because garages are not climate controlled and experience thermal cracking regularly. The crack of the stem wall (noted by an *X* in the lower left-hand corner) is a tie-down strap that is deteriorating and cracking the concrete stem wall. Installing piles on this house would have been a waste of time and money—and maybe even counterproductive.

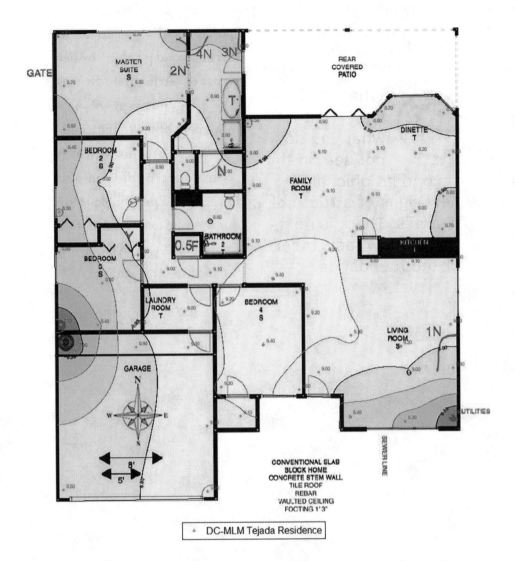

DC-MLM Tejada Residence

Figure 8.2: On this second reading (December 24, 2019), the high areas are in the same general locations but not as high.

After three years, the highest point measured is a small fraction of an inch lower. But what is more important is what you do not see on the second graphic: any new signs of structural distress. There is no sign of new movement of the foundation.

While it is instructive to compare the before and after images, we also are able to use our software to create a subtractive reading showing the change between the two readings.

> What is more important is what you do not see on the second graphic: any new signs of structural distress. There is no sign of new movement of the foundation.

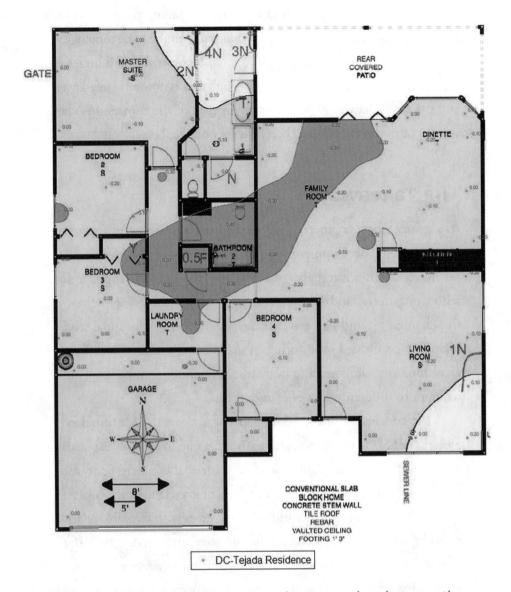

Figure 8.3: The subtractive topo map is a comparison between the original data points and those taken three years later.

Subtracting the elevation points of one reading from the other produces numerical values that can be plotted with the same topological software to produce the diagram above. In looking at this subtractive topo, it is easy to see that over time, the high area is now relatively lower, and the new relatively higher areas are in each of the corners. In other words, the dome has flattened by a little over one-half of an inch. Success!

The Takeaway

As a geotechnical engineer, Deatherage used a data-driven approach to evaluate the development, design, and results of the MoistureLevel System. His white paper was written in technical language for fellow engineers, and I have summarized only some highlights in this chapter. He and I agreed that the system merits additional study, including continued monitoring of installations, testing in different elevations and climates, and evaluating variations in the installation to adapt to different types of foundations.

The conclusion of the white paper was clear: the MoistureLevel System (MLS) "is an effective alternative measure to mitigate expansive soil dome heave under lightly loaded residential concrete floor slabs that have a several-inch-thick layer of ABC or gravel under the concrete floor. When used in climatic 'arid' and 'dry' areas with favorable relative humidity variations, the MLS can be effectively used to dry the surface of moist soils under concrete slabs during most times of the year. Depending on whether the subgrade soils are expansive clays that will shrink back when dried, or expansive clays that simply stop swelling when dried, the MLS can stop future clay heave, and in some cases cause the clay to shrink back and reduce the total dome heave."[3]

---

3   J. David Deatherage and Bob Brown, "Development and Engineering Aspects of the AZFS MoistureLevel Smart Foundation System."

* * *

Evaluating Previous Repairs

We are often asked to inspect a home where foundation repairs were performed previously, sometimes years earlier. Evaluating the success of those repairs is challenging in various ways.

If the homeowner doesn't know what repairs were done or even who did them, we might not be able to figure it out. Foundation repairs are hard to discover because they are below the surface. Even if there is some record of what repair was done, it may not accurately show where it was actually done. The original contractor may have produced a repair plan that shows what was proposed, but the actual work may have taken some unexpected turns. Getting an as-built plan that shows exactly what was installed where would be a real find.

Knowing whether the foundation was lifted makes a difference in analyzing the signs of stress such as cracks, sloped floors, and doors and windows out of square. If the foundation was raised up, and the contractor recorded floor-level readings before and after, we could evaluate the success of that repair work by taking new readings for comparison.

Finally, we would hope to see the damage prior to the repairs mapped with numbered photos corresponding to notations on the damage map. This documentation helps us see whether there are new signs of stress that were not present earlier or whether the preexisting signs of stress have worsened.

Let's take a look at examples showing what we could discover and show the homeowner whether all of this data is documented and available.

Figure 8.4

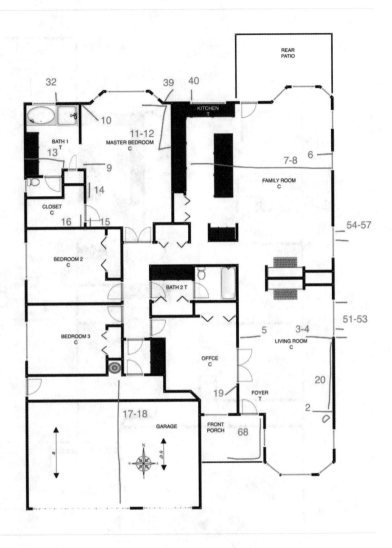

Figure 8.5

Even though the figure on the right identifies new signs of stress, many seem to match up with preexisting signs of stress on the left. The blue numbers correspond with photographs of damage for comparison between the current and previous reports.

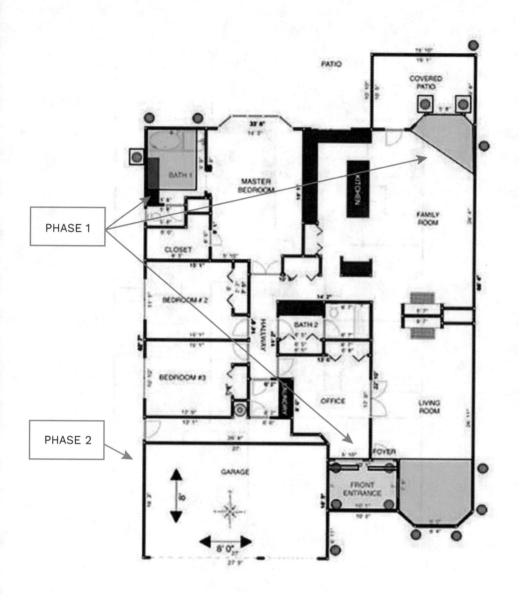

Figure 8.6

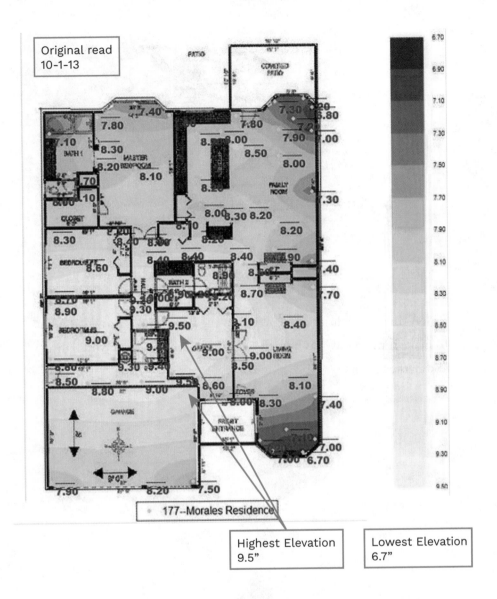

Figure 8.7

Repair plans and prework floor-level surveys help us evaluate the original repair plan. Here, lower elevations depicted with darker colors were underpinned, indicating that the original plan made sense from a data-driven analysis point of view.

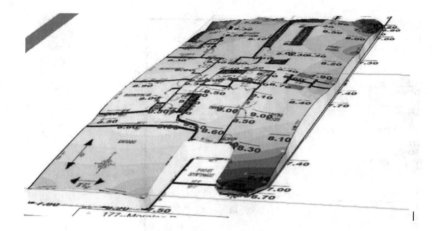

Figure 8.8

A three-dimensional depiction of the floor level is provided here to make it more obvious how the elevations are indicated with lighter and darker colors.

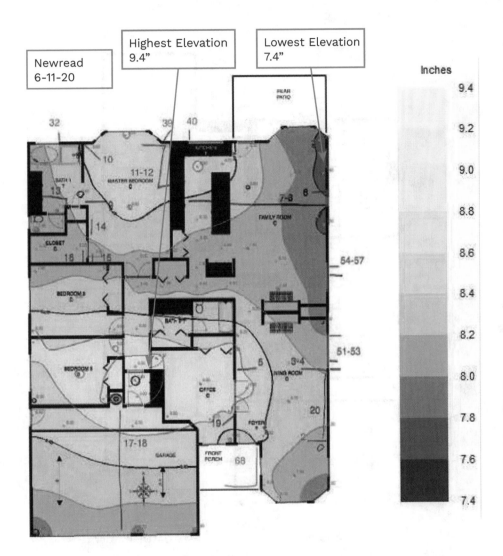

Figure 8.9: Later topo

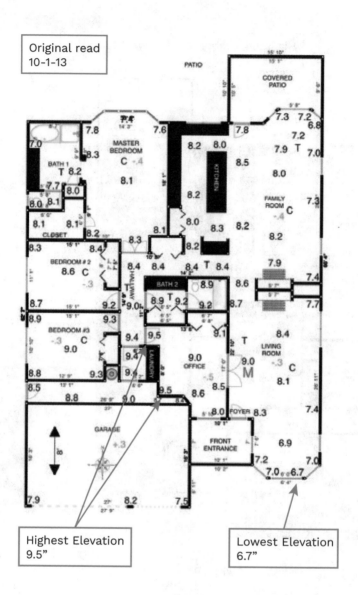

Figure 8.10

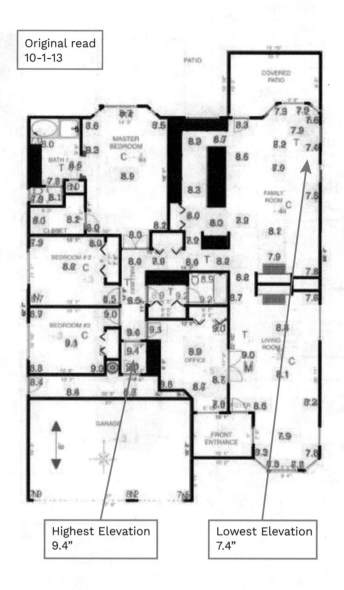

Original read
10-1-13

Highest Elevation
9.4"

Lowest Elevation
7.4"

Figure 8.11

This floor-level survey was taken nearly seven years after the original.

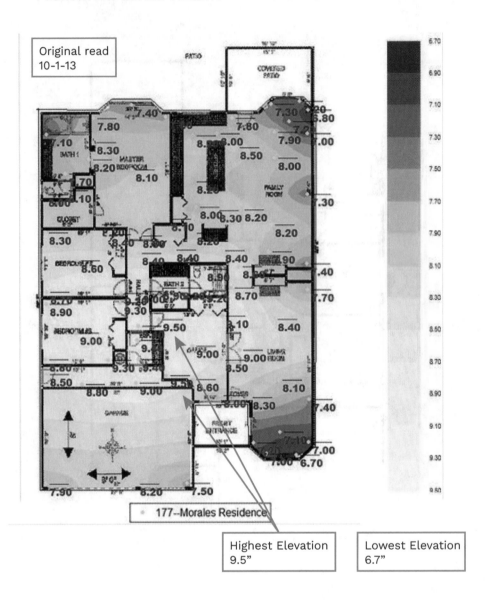

Figure 8.12

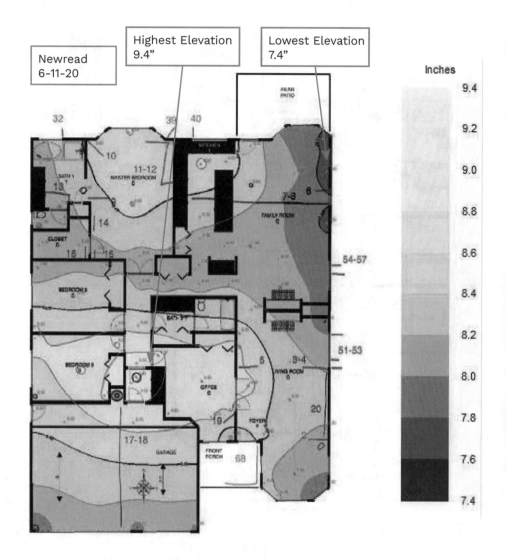

Figure 8.13

Looking at the two readings side by side, one notes that it is difficult to see any significant differences, even when they are rendered with topo software.

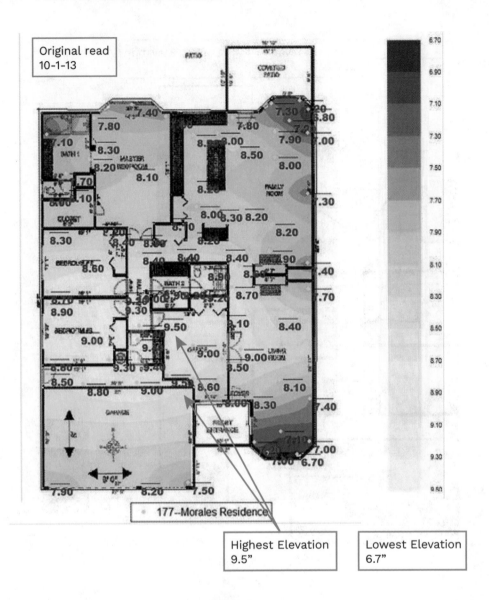

Figure 8.14

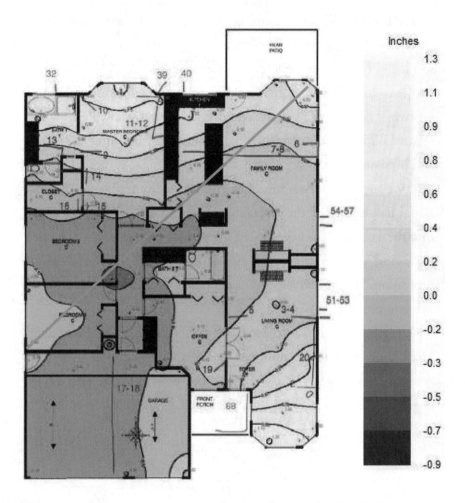

Figure 8.15

Subtracting the new data points from the corresponding original data points results in what we call a subtractive, depicted on the right. It shows how the elevations have changed over time. In this case, the former low areas are now relatively higher, indicating that those areas have been raised up.

These elevation readings reflect what happened in a home where piles were installed for underpinning. Because we could see that the areas raised up with underpinning are still relatively higher after seven years, and there were no substantial new signs of stress, the repair plan seemed to be performing as designed and intended.

Another degree of increased confidence could be gained if postwork floor-level readings could be obtained, showing how the relative floor levels changed in the timeframe from after the repair and present.

We could have even more confidence if a licensed design professional had examined the installation logs and affixed a seal to attest that the as-built plan was devised impartially and based on objective data. And we would have yet more confidence if a licensed design professional examined all of the comparative data and sealed his or her interpretation of it.

Not many contractors have this level of data from the original installation or have the ability to perform this kind of analysis. But when they do, a comparative analysis can be performed with a high degree of confidence about its conclusions. Otherwise? Good luck!

Now that you know what the MoistureLevel System can do, the next chapter addresses how to determine when it is a necessary and correct solution for your foundation problem.

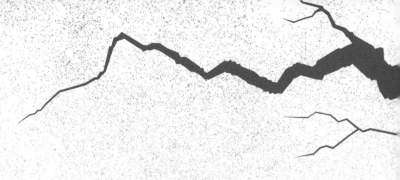

CHAPTER 9

WHY REMEDIATE A HEAVED SLAB?

Once we understand what slab heave is and what causes it, the question becomes "Why fix it?" Given all of the years it has been misdiagnosed and the lack of effective remedies in the past, a lot of homeowners have learned to live with it. They could take some comfort in being told that it was not a structural issue and that their house was not going to collapse or be condemned.

The most obvious reason for dealing with heave is that it creates tremendous dysfunctionality in the house. These "serviceability issues," as they are known in my profession, are very similar to foundation settlement problems. Examples are large cracks in the drywall, doors and windows that

The most obvious reason for dealing with heave is that it creates tremendous dysfunctionality in the house.

will not close properly, and floors with slopes and cracks. If the trusses start to lose their connections, then, under rare circumstances, the structure could become unstable.

If the homeowner wants to sell the house, the serviceability symptoms will be an issue. Potential buyers may greatly exaggerate their cost to remediate what they could mistakenly assume is foundation settlement.

Some of the serviceability issues have direct consequences. Doors that don't close properly waste energy. Gaps allow pests to enter. Floor coverings must be replaced. I have seen floors develop cracks as much as two inches wide.

Now or Later?

If you have evidence of floor heave from expansive soils, and the serviceability issues are not dire, what are the pros and cons of fixing now versus later?

The big justification for waiting is that you don't have a structural deficiency. The floating slab in a conventional foundation is generally not considered a structural component of the house because it is not connected to the perimeter footing. An engineer would tell you that movement or cracking in the slab would not, by definition, be a structural issue because the roof load of the house is still safely supported from below. A rare exception to this is when the floor slab heaving pushes up so high that it puts pressure on the trusses on the bottom side from the interior walls—that can be a structural problem.

"If it is not a structural problem, why bother fixing it?" is the wrong question. The question should be "Have the serviceability issues been handled in such a manner that it creates credibility for future buyers?"

Issues such as cracking of the interior walls and floors along with doors that will not function need to be dealt with before a sale. No one would want to buy a house with those issues. But if the seller must disclose that the repairs were done a few weeks ago, that is not reassuring. The homeowner does not have any credible evidence to support future performance other than the claims of the repair contractor.

Even if the repair contractor has a good reputation and provides a lifetime warranty, the buyer is going to be wary. But if a few years have passed since the repairs, and the seller can say there have been no issues, it shows the work has stood the test of time. The sooner the repairs are done, the greater the credibility.

Proper documentation helps establish the fact that the condition has been dealt with in a proactive manner that will not result in future problems. And of course, the homeowner should be sure the work was done with a permit. Sometimes a real estate agent will call me in to evaluate how past underpinning has performed on a house for sale. But with no documentation of what work was done, and no data on where things stood immediately before and after the repairs, I can't tell how those repairs are performing. I can only evaluate its current state. I wish more people in my industry appreciated that need.

By controlling the moisture under the slab and managing it in a proactive way, we prevent a small heave from developing into a large heave.

Specifically, in the case of floor heave, if we control the moisture under the slab and manage it in a proactive way, we prevent a small heave from developing into a large heave. The MoistureLevel® Smart Foundation System is comparatively less expensive than other alternatives. It should be used to prevent serviceability issues and avoid giving future buyers the mistaken impression that the house has a structural problem.

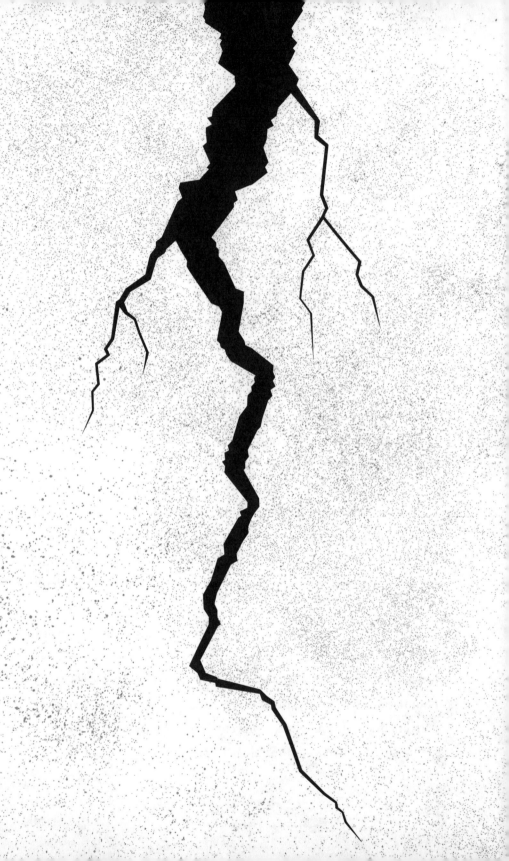

CONCLUSION

THE NEED FOR HEAVE MITIGATION

I have explained how the different types of soil affect common foundation systems and how most foundation problems in an arid and semiarid climate result from heave and not settlement. I also established that many—I estimate up to half of—foundation problems get misdiagnosed by contractors and even some engineers. I showed how the typical industry methods for remediating heave misdiagnosed as settlement are wrong and counterproductive and how the traditional repair methods that do work on heave are expensive, impractical, and not very effective in the long run.

I detailed the due diligence required to properly diagnose a failing foundation. Without going through that hard work, mistakes are likely to happen. Of course, if the investigation is done solely by a commissioned salesperson, the chances of the analysis being objective and thorough are very low—especially if the sale depends on using methods that fix only one type of problem. If the only tool you have is a hammer, then all of your problems start looking like nails!

In the final chapters, I discussed a revolutionary new way to mitigate the effects of expansive clays on existing foundations and floor slabs. I have developed this method and patented it so that I can have something of value to offer homeowners and building owners with this difficult-to-resolve problem. It is a unique, non-intrusive solution that has had very good results. In my discussions with geotechnical engineers and structural engineers, I have received supportive and encouraging comments for the system—with very few naysayers.

The concepts in this book change the way we think about, analyze, and repair foundations, especially in areas of high clay content and arid or semiarid climate.

At Arizona Foundation Solutions, we have installed about two thousand MoistureLevel® systems, proving the demand exists for a cost-effective and proactive method of remediating heave. The MoistureLevel System runs only about 5 percent of the cost typically charged for very intrusive and minimally effective heave mitigation treatments. Not only is it one-twentieth of the cost, but it produces far superior results! At the same time, it mitigates cancer-causing radon and other harmful gases (volatile organic compounds and PCBs from pollution), eliminates the problem of wet slabs, and reduces moisture under the slab, which is what termites are attracted to.

 The Moisture-Level System runs only about 5 percent of the cost typically charged for very intrusive and minimally effective heave mitigation treatments. Not only is it one-twentieth of the cost, but it produces far superior results!

I wrote this book partly to encourage homeowners to recognize that many heave-related problems can be prevented with proper moisture management under the slab. A good interactive system will maintain the proper moisture content and prevent clays from swelling and causing much greater future problems. The other big reason I wrote this book was to help homeowners arm themselves with how foundation repairs should be developed. The book also was intended as a guide for homeowners to better understand the enigmas of foundation repair in order to more productively interact with foundation repair companies. You can read more on my author's website and blog at www.foundationrepairsecrets.com. I hope it proves useful to many people.